SECRETS OF
French
Hors d'Oeuvres

OVER 100 AUTHENTIC RECIPES

General Editor · Beverly LeBlanc

Macdonald Orbis

A Macdonald Orbis BOOK

Based upon *Grand Livre de la Cuisine,* © Edition No 1, Paris 1982
English text and design © Macdonald & Co (Publishers) Ltd 1986, 1988

First published in Great Britain in 1988
by Macdonald & Co (Publishers) Ltd
London & Sydney

A member of BPCC plc

British Library Cataloguing in Publication Data

Secrets of French hors d'oeuvres
1. Cookery (appetizers)
I. LeBlanc, Beverly
641.8'12   TX 740

ISBN 0-356-15580-3

Illustrated by Alison Wisenfeld

Editor: Jennifer Jones
Designer: Clair Lidzey
Indexer: Myra Clark

Printed and bound in Great Britain by
Purnell Book Production Ltd, Paulton, Bristol
A member of BPCC plc

Macdonald & Co (Publishers) Ltd
Greater London House
Hampstead Road
London NW1 7QX

CONTENTS

Symbols

The symbols show how easy a recipe is, and the preparation and cooking times:

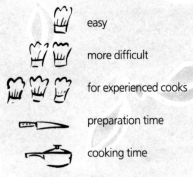

easy

more difficult

for experienced cooks

preparation time

cooking time

When using this book, remember the following points: (1) all quantities are for four people, unless otherwise stated; (2) use only one set of ingredients for the recipes, since American imperial and metric measurements are not exact equivalents and (3) in the text of recipes, American quantities and ingredients are listed first, with the British equivalents in square brackets.

INTRODUCTION

Traditionally, an hors d'oeuvre is served as an appetizer dish at the beginning of a meal, and it can consist of anything from a few raw vegetables lightly dressed to something more elaborate like stuffed crêpes or vol-au-vents. Hors d'oeuvres can also form part of a buffet, be served up as party pieces, and some of the more substantial hors d'oeuvres found in this book might also provide the answer as to what to serve for a light lunch or supper dish. Clearly, hors d'oeuvres have a place in every cook's repertoire.

Part of the secret of successful hors d'oeuvres is in the preparation, particularly when it comes to vegetables. To start off the cold hors d'oeuvres section, there are clear instructions on how to prepare vegetables for such simple yet delicious dishes as Artichoke Vinaigrette, Raw Vegetable Platter and Celeriac in Mayonnaise. This also applies to salads, which follow next. The French know that a good salad need not necessarily be fussy or complicated. Some of the most delicious salads are also the simplest when served with a basic, well-made dressing. However, whether you prefer to present the salad as a first course or after the main dish to aid the digestion, it should always be made with the freshest of ingredients, well tossed in dressing and served immediately. This last point is important: a salad that is left to stand in its dressing for any length of time quickly becomes limp and unappetizing.

A section on terrines, pâtés and galantines – the heart of many a buffet – is followed by hot hors d'oeuvres ranging from *amuse-gueules,* such as Cheese and Sausage Brioches, Chicken Vol-au-Vents and Roquefort Puffs to more substantial offerings, such as crêpes, soufflés, tarts and pies. And to close, there is a small selection of, mainly classic French, recipes for soups that will be particularly welcome on a cold winter's evening.

These recipes from the French kitchen offer dishes for every occasion, and for every level of expertise. Enjoy them—and *bon appétit!*

COLD HORS D'OEUVRES

Preparing raw vegetables

Asparagus

Hold the asparagus spear with its tip toward you. Using a swivel-bladed vegetable peeler and working towards the base of the spear, carefully peel away the outer skin.

Cabbage

With a large pointed knife, slice the cabbage in two and cut away the woody core of each half.

Endive (chicory) heart

Insert a small sharp knife at the base of the head to a depth of ¾ in / 2 cm, and cut out the cone formed by the center leaves.

Fennel and celery

Remove the leafy green part of the celery stalk or fennel bulb, then pull off any tough fibers or strings with a paring knife.

Garlic clove

Place the clove under the flat surface of a kitchen knife and press down firmly. This will flatten the garlic and burst the outer skin, which will then come away easily. Remove the outer skin and crush the garlic in a garlic press, or using a mortar and pestle.

Globe artichoke hearts

Cut off the stalk with a stainless steel knife. Pull the thick outside leaves away. Remove the choke with a grapefruit knife or a teaspoon and rub the cut surface of the heart with a slice of lemon to prevent discoloration.

Green beans

Make a cut across one end of the bean without severing it completely. Catching the string with the blade of your knife, pull it away along the bean's length. Repeat at the other end to remove the string from the other side.

Pumpkin

Cut the pumpkin into quarters and peel away its skin with a small sharp knife. Remove and discard the seeds and the coarse stringy material inside.

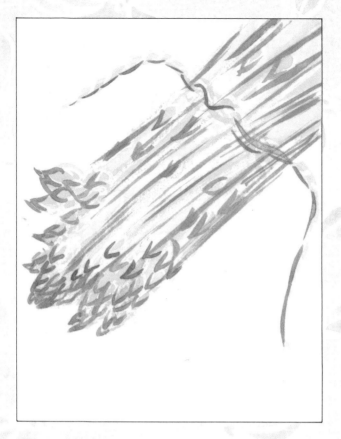

Tomatoes

Cut out the hard, green core around the stalk, then immerse the tomatoes in boiling water for 10 seconds if they are ripe, a little longer if they are not. The skins will then slip off easily. Cut in half to scoop or press out the seeds.

Leeks

Remove any roots, cut off the damaged ends of the green leaves and slice the leek lengthwise into quarters. Holding the leaves open, wash each section thoroughly under cold running water.

Shallots

Cut a thin slice from each end of the shallot, then remove and discard the papery skin and the first fleshy layer.

Spinach and sorrel leaves

Fold the leaf in two along the central stalk. Hold the folded leaf in one hand, and with the other tear the stalk away working from the base to the tip.

Sweet pepper (capsicum)

Cut the pepper in half lengthwise and remove the core, seeds and whitish membrane.

Artichauts vinaigrette

Artichokes Vinaigrette

	00:10	00:25 to 00:30

American	Ingredients	Metric/Imperial
6	Globe artichokes	6
	Salt and pepper	
1 tbsp	Vinegar	1 tbsp
1 tbsp	Prepared mustard, preferably Dijon	1 tbsp
3 tbsp	Oil	3 tbsp
1	Fresh parsley sprig	1

1. Break off the stalks of the artichokes, pulling them to remove the strings also. Remove any damaged leaves.
2. Bring a large saucepan of salted water to a boil. Add the artichokes and leave to cook for about 30 minutes. To test if they are done, pull out one of the large leaves near the base. If it comes out easily, the artichokes are ready.
3. Remove the artichokes from the water, and drain.
4. For the dressing, dissolve a pinch of salt in the vinegar. Stir in the mustard. Season with pepper to taste. Add the oil and chopped parsley and mix thoroughly.
5. Serve the vinaigrette with the warm or cold artichokes.

Caviar d'aubergines

Eggplant [Aubergine] Caviar

	00:20 plus chilling	00:35

American	Ingredients	Metric/Imperial
2	Eggplant [aubergines]	2
1	Large, very firm tomato	1
1	Shallot	1
1	Garlic clove (optional)	1
	Salt and pepper	
⅔ cup	Olive oil	150 ml / ¼ pint
1 tbsp	Chopped fresh dill or parsley	1 tbsp

1. Preheat the oven to 350°F / 180°C / Gas Mark 4.
2. Place the whole eggplant in the oven and bake until the skin becomes cracked and the eggplant are soft to the touch. Remove them from the oven and peel.
3. Peel the tomato (first plunging it in boiling water for 10 seconds), remove the seeds and cut into pieces.
4. Mince the eggplant and tomato purée in a blender or food processor until smooth.
5. Peel the shallot and garlic. Crush them in a mortar or blend to a purée.
6. Put all the puréed ingredients into a salad bowl and add salt and pepper to taste. Stir with a wooden spoon, gradually adding the olive oil in a trickle as for mayonnaise. You should obtain a thick paste. Chill lightly.
7. Add the chopped dill or parsley just before serving.

Assiette de crudités

Raw Vegetable Platter

	00:40 to 00:50	00:10
	plus infusing	

American	Ingredients	Metric/Imperial
2 tbsp	Cider vinegar	2 tbsp
½ cup	Oil	125 ml / 4 fl oz
2	Canned anchovy fillets	2
1 tbsp	Chopped fresh chives	1 tbsp
1 tbsp	Chopped fresh tarragon	1 tbsp
1	Small cauliflower	1
1	Head of red cabbage	1
6	Carrots	6
1	Head of celery	1
2	Cooked beets [beetroot]	2
1	Bunch of radishes	1
¾ lb	Mushrooms	350 g / 12 oz
1	Lemon	1
6	Eggs	6
	Salt and pepper	

1. About 2 hours before serving, prepare the vinaigrette. Mix the cider vinegar and oil in a bowl. Pound the anchovy fillets to a cream in a mortar with a pestle. Add to the oil and vinegar with the chives and tarragon. Leave to infuse for 2 hours, stirring occasionally. Do not add salt and pepper until you are ready to serve.

2. Break the cauliflower into florets. Core the red cabbage, and cut it into thin strips. Peel the carrots and grate them finely. Trim the celery and cut into small cubes. Peel the beets and dice them. Trim the radishes, leaving some of the leaves on them. Thinly slice the mushrooms, then sprinkle them with the juice of the lemon to keep them white.

3. Arrange all the vegetables on a large serving dish.

4. Hard-cook the eggs for 10 minutes in boiling water. Run them under cold water to cool, and remove the shells.

5. Cut the pointed tip off each egg. Remove the yolk from the cut-off pieces and crush it finely with a fork. Add the crushed yolk to the vinaigrette and season with salt and pepper. Decorate the serving dish with the rest of the eggs.

6. Serve the vegetables accompanied by the vinaigrette in a sauceboat.

Asperges à la flamande

Asparagus, Flemish Style

00:30   00:30 to 00:45

American	Ingredients	Metric/Imperial
3 lb	Asparagus	1.5 kg / 3 lb
3	Eggs	3
2 tbsp	Chopped fresh chervil or parsley	2 tbsp
2 tbsp	Chopped fresh chives	2 tbsp
	Salt and pepper	
1 cup	Butter	250 g / 8 oz
1	Lemon	1

1. Trim the woody ends from the asparagus, then scrape the stalks. Tie the asparagus spears in 3 equal bunches. Set aside.

2. Hard-cook the eggs for 10 minutes in a saucepan of boiling water. Drain and cool, then shell the eggs. Chop them finely, or blend briefly in a blender or food processor. Add the chervil and chives and mix well.

3. Put salted water on to boil in a large saucepan. When the water is boiling, add the bunches of asparagus. As soon as the water returns to a boil, reduce the heat to keep the water simmering. Leave to cook for 5-20 minutes (depending on the age and size of the asparagus) or until tender.

4. Meanwhile, heat the butter in a heatproof glass bowl placed in a saucepan of simmering water (or use a double boiler). As soon as the butter has melted, remove the bowl from the pan and allow to cool. After a moment or two, a white sediment will form on the bottom of the bowl. Pour the clear melted butter very gently from the top into a serving bowl, leaving the sediment behind.

5. Add the juice of the lemon to the clarified butter. Add salt and pepper to taste. Stir in one-quarter of the egg and herb mixture.

6. Drain the asparagus and arrange on a warmed serving dish. Sprinkle with the remaining egg and herb mixture. Serve warm, accompanied by the butter sauce.

Concombres à la crème

Cucumbers in Cream

	00:20 plus draining and chilling	00:00

American	Ingredients	Metric/Imperial
2	Cucumbers	2
	Salt and pepper	
10	Fresh tarragon sprigs	10
2	Lemons	2
1 cup	Crème fraîche	250 ml / 8 fl oz

1. Wipe the cucumbers and cut into thin slices. Place the slices in a colander and sprinkle with salt. Stir and leave to drain for 30 minutes.
2. Rinse the cucumber slices in cold water and drain again. Pat the slices dry with paper towels.
3. Chop the leaves from the tarragon sprigs and put in a salad bowl with the juice from the 2 lemons. Add pepper to taste. Gradually stir in the crème fraîche.
4. Add the cucumber slices and fold together gently. Chill well.
5. Serve very cold, garnished with a few leaves of tarragon.

Céleri rémoulade

Celeriac in Mayonnaise

	00:20 plus marinating	00:00

American	Ingredients	Metric/Imperial
1 (1 lb)	Head of celeriac	1 (500 g / 1 lb)
1	Lemon	1
	Salt and pepper	
1	Egg yolk	1
2 tbsp	Strong prepared mustard	2 tbsp
1 tbsp	Vinegar	1 tbsp
1 cup	Oil	250 ml / 8 fl oz
2 tbsp	Chopped fresh parsley	2 tbsp

1. Peel the celeriac and sprinkle it with the juice of half the lemon so that it does not discolor. Grate it coarsely.
2. Place the celeriac in a bowl and sprinkle with the remaining lemon juice in which you have dissolved ½ teaspoon of salt. Leave to blanch for 30 minutes to 1 hour, stirring occasionally.
3. Meanwhile, place the egg yolk in a bowl and add the mustard, vinegar, and salt and pepper to taste. Mix well. Gradually add the oil, whisking vigorously. The mayonnaise must be quite thick and adhere to the whisk. If it is too thick, add a little more vinegar.
4. Drain the celeriac, squeezing it in your hand, and place in a salad bowl. Add the mayonnaise gradually, stirring to combine the ingredients thoroughly.
5. Leave to stand for 30 minutes before serving, sprinkled with chopped parsley.

Avocats garnis

Stuffed Avocado

	00:30		00:00

American	Ingredients	Metric/Imperial
3	Avocados	3
	Lemon juice	
	Salt and pepper	
1	Celery stalk	1
6	Lettuce leaves	6
1 cup	Black olives	150 g / 5 oz

1. Cut the avocados in half lengthwise and remove the seed. Brush the cut surfaces with lemon juice to prevent the from discoloring. Season the avocados with salt and pepper to taste.
2. Trim and dice the celery. Place each avocado half on a lettuce leaf, surrounded by a few olives and a little diced celery. Fill the hollows in the avocado halves with one of the following preparations:

Anchovy vinaigrette: prepare a vinaigrette dressing and season it to taste with anchovy paste or essence. Garnish the avocado with a few rolled anchovy fillets.

Shrimp: allow 1 tablespoon cooked peeled shrimp [prawns], a little diced celery and 1 tablespoon mayonnaise for each avocado half. Season with a few drops of tabasco sauce.

Crab: as for shrimp, using canned or freshly cooked crab meat, and decorate with a few black olives.

Tuna: allow 1 tablespoon flaked canned tuna and a little diced celery dressed with vinaigrette or mayonnaise for each half avocado.

Crudités aux poivrons

Raw Vegetables with Pimiento Paste

	00:45		00:10

American	Ingredients	Metric/Imperial
1	Cucumber	1
	Salt	
4	Potatoes	4
4	Eggs	4
4	Tomatoes	4
1	Head of celery	1
½	Can of pimientos	½
1½ tsp	Chopped fresh chervil or parsley	1½ tsp
1 cup	Mayonnaise	250 ml / 8 fl oz
	Toast for serving	

1. Wipe the cucumber and cut it into thin slices. Place in a colander, sprinkle with salt and leave to drain for 1 hour. Rinse under cold water, drain again and pat dry with paper towels.
2. Rinse the potatoes and put them unpeeled into a saucepan

of cold salted water. Bring to a boil and leave to cook for about 20 minutes or until tender. Drain in a colander. When cool enough to handle, peel the potatoes and dice them.

3. Hard-cook the eggs in boiling water for 10 minutes. Drain and remove the shells.

4. Thinly slice the tomatoes. Trim and dice the celery. Drain the pimientos and pat dry with paper towels.

5. Purée the pimientos with the hard-cooked eggs in a blender or food processor until smooth . Add the chervil and mix it in, then add 1 tablespoon of the mayonnaise.

6. Put the pimiento paste into a cup in the middle of a serving dish, and surround with the raw vegetables. Serve with toast, which your guests will spread with pimiento paste instead of butter, and with the remaining mayonnaise — flavored, if liked, with chopped fresh herbs. You can replace the mayonnaise with a vinaigrette dressing.

Thyme

Tomates farcies

Stuffed Tomatoes

American	Ingredients	Metric/Imperial
6	Ripe tomatoes	6
	Salt and pepper	
3	Fresh parsley sprigs	3
1	Fresh thyme sprig	1
1	Onion	1
1	Garlic clove	1
1½ cups	Ground [minced] cooked meat (beef, veal, etc)	350 g / 12 oz
1	Slice of bread	1
½ cup	Milk	125 ml / 4 fl oz
1	Egg	1
	Pinch of grated nutmeg	

1. Preheat the oven to 350°F / 180°C / Gas Mark 4.

2. Cut the tops off the tomatoes, and reserve them. Scoop the flesh and seeds out of the tomatoes using a small spoon. Season the insides of the tomatoes with salt and pepper, then leave them to drain, unside-down, on paper towels for 15 minutes.

3. Finely chop or mince the parsley, thyme, peeled onion and garlic. Place these ingredients in a mixing bowl and add the meat.

4. Soak the bread in the milk. Squeeze out excess milk, then add the bread to the bowl. Add the egg, nutmeg and salt and pepper to taste. Mix thoroughly.

5. Fill the tomatoes with the meat mixture and replace the tops. Arrange in a baking dish and bake for about 30 minutes. Serve hot or cold.

Garlic, parsley, thyme, mint, bay leaf and coriander seeds

Coeurs d'artichaut à la provençale

Artichoke Hearts Provençal Style

🔪	00:15		01:00 🥘

American	Ingredients	Metric/Imperial
36	Small purple globe artichokes	36
1	Lemon	1
4	Tomatoes	4
12	Pearl [button] onions	12
½ lb	Lightly salted bacon	250 g / 8 oz
6 tbsp	Olive oil	6 tbsp
1 tsp	Chopped fresh thyme	1 tsp
2	Bay leaves	2
	Salt and pepper	
1 tbsp	Chopped fresh basil	1 tbsp

1. Break off the artichoke stalks. Cut away the small outside leaves. Sprinkle the juice of half the lemon over the outside of the artichoke hearts so that they do not turn black. Continue cutting away all the side leaves, leaving only the center ones. Cut off the center leaves at their base. Completely remove the hairy choke, leaving the heart clean. Sprinkle with the remaining lemon juice.

2. Quarter and core the tomatoes. Peel the onions. Dice the bacon.

3. Place the bacon in a heavy saucepan and heat until it renders its fat. Drain the bacon on paper towels. Pour off the fat from the pan.

4. Heat the olive oil in a saucepan. Add the artichoke hearts, thyme and bay leaves cut into thin strips and cook until the artichoke hearts are lightly browned. Add the onions and brown lightly, turning them to cook evenly.

5. Return the bacon to the pan with the tomatoes, and salt and pepper to taste. Cover and leave to cook over a low heat for about 1 hour.

6. About 15 minutes before cooking is finished, add the basil. Serve hot or cold.

Feuilles de vigne farcies

Stuffed Grape Leaves

01:00
plus cooling

01:00

American	Ingredients	Metric/Imperial
36	Grape or vine leaves	36
1¼ cups	Water	300 ml / ½ pint
	Salt and pepper	
¾ cup	Long-grain rice	150 g / 5 oz
6	Onions	6
1	Garlic clove	1
5 tbsp	Olive oil	5 tbsp
5	Fresh parsley sprigs	5
4 - 5	Fresh mint leaves	4 - 5
10	Coriander seeds	10
2	Bay leaves	2
1	Lemon	1

1. Plunge the grape leaves into boiling water, then drain and spread out on a cloth. Set aside.

2. Bring the water to a boil with salt to taste. Add the rice and simmer for 12 minutes: the rice should still be slightly crisp.

3. Meanwhile, peel and finely chop the onions and garlic. Heat 2 tablespoons of the oil in a saucepan, add the onions and garlic and cook over a very gentle heat until softened but not browned. Chop the parsley and mint leaves and add to the saucepan. Stir quickly over the heat.

4. Remove from the heat and add the rice. Season to taste with pepper and mix thoroughly.

5. Preheat the oven to 400°F / 200°C / Gas Mark 6.

6. Place a little pile of the rice mixture on each grape leaf. Fold over the sides, then roll up the leaf into a rather tight sausage.

7. Place the rolled leaves in an ovenproof dish. Cover with cold water and add the remaining olive oil, the coriander seeds and halved bay leaves. Put a plate on the rolled leaves to keep them submerged in the water.

8. Bake about 45 minutes or until the rice has absorbed most of the liquid, and you can pierce the rolls very easily with the point of a knife.

9. Remove the dish from the oven and leave to cool.

10. Drain the rolled grape leaves when cold. Squeeze the juice from half the lemon over the rolled leaves and garnish with the remaining lemon, thinly sliced.

Asperges sauce mousseline

Asparagus with Mousseline Sauce

🔪 00:20   00:35 🥘

American	Ingredients	Metric/Imperial
3 lb	Asparagus	1.5 kg / 3 lb
⅔ cup	Vinegar	150 ml / ¼ pint
6	Black peppercorns	6
	Salt	
2	Egg yolks	2
6 tbsp	Butter	75 g / 3 oz
⅔ cup	Heavy [double] cream	150 ml / ¼ pint

1. Trim the woody ends from the asparagus, then scrape the stalks. Tie the asparagus spears in 4 equal bunches, and set aside.

2. Place the vinegar and peppercorns in a small saucepan and bring to a boil. Boil until reduced to 1 tablespoon.

3. Meanwhile, put salted water on to boil in a large saucepan. When the water is boiling, add the bunches of asparagus. As soon as boiling resumes, reduce the heat to keep the water simmering. Leave to cook for 5-20 minutes (depending on the age and size of the asparagus) or until tender.

4. When the asparagus is cooked, remove it from the water and drain well. Arrange on a folded napkin on a warmed serving dish and keep hot.

5. Strain the peppercorns from the reduced vinegar. Remove the pan from the heat and add the egg yolks, whisking vigorously. Gradually incorporate the butter, cut into small pieces, continuing to whisk until thickened. Add salt to taste.

6. Whip the cream until thick and fold into the sauce.

7. Serve the mousseline sauce in a sauceboat with the asparagus.

Fonds d'artichaut vinaigrette

Artichoke Hearts Vinaigrette

🔪 00:20   00:30 🥘

American	Ingredients	Metric/Imperial
6	Large globe artichokes	6
	Salt and pepper	
3 tbsp	Chopped fresh chives	3 tbsp
	Lemon juice	
6	Eggs	6
2½ tbsp	Cider vinegar	2½ tbsp
1 tsp	Strong prepared mustard	1 tsp
⅔ cup	Oil	150 ml / ¼ pint
6	Tomatoes	6
1	Head of celery	1
1¼ cups	Black olives	400 g / 14 oz

1. Cook the artichokes in boiling salted water for 10 minutes. Drain upside-down.

2. Remove the artichoke leaves, keeping the hearts intact. Remove the hairy choke and set the hearts aside. Grate the flesh from the base of the leaves. Discard the leaves.

3. Mix the grated artichoke flesh with the chives and a few drops of lemon juice. Spread the mixture over the artichoke hearts.

4. Hard-cook the eggs in boiling water. Drain and remove the shells. Halve the eggs.

5. Dissolve a pinch of salt in the cider vinegar. Mix the mustard with the vinegar. Add the oil and pepper to taste, mixing thoroughly.

6. Serve each artichoke heart on a separate plate together with a quartered tomato, 2 egg halves, a few sticks of celery and olives. Serve the vinaigrette in a sauceboat.

Oignons à l'orientale

Sweet and Sour Onions

00:20 plus cooling   00:40

American	Ingredients	Metric/Imperial
2 lb	Small onions of the same size	1 kg / 2 lb
¼ cup	Tomato paste [purée]	4 tbsp
10	White peppercorns	10
20	Coriander seeds	20
1	Bouquet garni	1
1 tbsp	Sugar or	1 tbsp
⅔ cup	Raisins	125 g / 4 oz
	Paprika	
1	Lemon	1
3 cups	Dry white wine	750 ml / 1 ¼ pints
¼ cup	Olive oil	4 tbsp
1 cup	Water	250 ml / 8 fl oz
	Salt	

1. Peel the onions and drop them into boiling water. Simmer for 5 minutes, then drain.

2. Place the onions in a saucepan and add the tomato paste, peppercorns, coriander seeds, bouquet garni, sugar or raisins and a pinch of paprika. Add the juice of the lemon, the wine, olive oil and water. Add salt to taste.

3. Bring to a boil and leave to simmer until the onions are tender (35-45 minutes, depending on size). When ready, the onions should be coated in the sauce which has reduced. If there is too much sauce, remove the onions and boil to reduce it still further over a brisk heat.

4. Allow to cool, and discard the bouquet garni before serving.

Cook's tip: mushrooms can be prepared in the same way, but add the juice of 2 lemons.

Pan bagnat

Provençal Sandwiches

⌧ 00:10
plus peeling peppers
00:10 to 00:15

American	Ingredients	Metric/Imperial
6	Small loaves of french bread or rolls	6
2 cups	Olive oil	500 ml / ¾ pint
3	Garlic cloves (optional)	3
3	Sweet red or green peppers	3
6	Small tomatoes	6
6	Medium-size onions	6
24	Black olives	24
1	Bunch of radishes	1
12 - 18	Canned anchovy fillets in oil	12 - 18

1. Preheat the oven to 450°F / 230°C / Gas Mark 8.

2. Cut the loaves or rolls in half and brush the cut surfaces generously with the olive oil. Peel and crush the garlic and sprinkle over the bread.

3. Place the peppers in the oven and bake until the skin blisters. Rub the peppers in a damp cloth and the skin will come off without any difficulty. Halve the peppers and remove the core and seeds. Cut the peppers into strips.

4. Slice the tomatoes. Peel the onions and cut into rings. Pit [stone] the olives, and trim and slice the radishes.

5. Top one half of each loaf or roll with tomato slices, onion rings, pepper strips, 2-3 drained anchovy fillets, 4 olives and radish slices. Cover with the other half of the loaf or roll and wrap tightly in foil. Set aside for a few minutes, even if you are to eat the sandwiches immediately.

Tapenade

Olive, Anchovy and Caper Spread

🔪 00:25   00:00 🫕

American	Ingredients	Metric/Imperial
1½ cups	Large black olives	250 g / 8 oz
4 oz	Canned anchovy fillets	125 g / 4 oz
1½ tbsp	Capers	1½ tbsp
1¼ cups	Olive oil	300 ml / ½ pint
1	Lemon	1
	Salt and pepper	

1. Pit [stone] the olives, then put them into a food processor or blender with the anchovies and capers. Blend to a smooth cream.
2. Pour and scrape the mixture into a bowl. Gradually beat in the olive oil as if making mayonnaise, adding a few drops of lemon juice from time to time. Season with salt and pepper to taste.
3. Cover and keep in a cool place, in a tight-sealed container, until ready to serve.
4. Serve as a dip, or spread on small savory crackers [biscuits] or slices of french bread and sprinkle with a few more drops of lemon juice.

Citrons farcis au thon

Lemons with Tuna

🔪 00:30
plus chilling   00:00 🫕

American	Ingredients	Metric/Imperial
6	Large, thick-skinned lemons	6
1 (7 oz)	Can of tuna	1 (200 g / 7 oz)
1	Egg yolk	1
1 tsp	Prepared mustard	1 tsp
1 cup	Oil	250 ml / 8 fl oz
1 tbsp	Vinegar	1 tbsp
	Salt and pepper	
	Tabasco sauce (optional)	
6	Black olives	6

1. Cut off the pointed ends of the lemons and scrape out the pulp using a small spoon. Do not pierce the lemon skins. Set aside the lemon shells and cut-off ends.
2. Cut the lemon pulp into cubes and place these in a mixing bowl. Drain and flake the tuna and add to the diced lemon.
3. Place the egg yolk in another bowl with the mustard and add the oil gradually in a trickle, blending with a whisk. When the mayonnaise is quite firm, incorporate the vinegar and season with salt, pepper and a few drops of tabasco sauce.
4. Add the mayonnaise to the tuna mixture and stir well. Stuff the lemon shells with the tuna mayonnaise. Garnish with olives and cover with the cut-off ends of the lemons. Chill until ready to serve.

Tomatoes fourrées au thon

Tomatoes Stuffed with Tuna

	00:30		00:10	
	plus chilling			

American	Ingredients	Metric/Imperial
6	Medium-size tomatoes	6
	Salt and pepper	
1 lb	Fresh peas in their shells	500 g / 1 lb
1 (3½ oz)	Can of tuna in brine	1 (75 g / 3 oz)
7	Garlic cloves	7
1 cup	Olive oil	250 ml / 8 fl oz
2	Egg yolks	2
2½ - 3 tbsp	Lemon juice	2½ - 3 tbsp
1 tbsp	Chopped fresh parsley	1 tbsp

1. Wipe the tomatoes. Cut off the tops and put to one side. Empty out the insides using a small spoon. Remove and discard the seeds from the flesh which you have taken out. Chop the flesh, add salt and pepper to taste and put to one side.
2. Shell the peas. Toss them into a saucepan of boiling salted water, bring back to a boil, and leave to cook for 2 minutes. Drain in a colander and run under cold water to chill.
3. Drain the tuna in a strainer and flake it.
4. Peel and crush the garlic in a mortar. Add 1-2 tablespoons of the olive oil and reduce to a paste. Add the egg yolks and mix well. Tip into a mixing bowl and add the rest of the oil in a trickle, whisking constantly until thickened to a mayonnaise. Add the lemon juice, salt and pepper to taste and mix well.
5. Mix the tuna, peas and tomato flesh. Fold in the garlic mayonnaise.
6. Fill the tomatoes with the tuna mixture and sprinkle each with chopped parsley. Replace the tops and serve the tomatoes lightly chilled.

Aspics de foies de volaille

Chicken Livers in Aspic

	00:20		00:08	
	plus chilling			

American	Ingredients	Metric/Imperial
1	Shallot	1
3 tbsp	Butter	40 g / 1½ oz
1 lb	Chicken livers	500 g / 1 lb
	Salt and pepper	
	Dried thyme	
1 tbsp	Cognac	1 tbsp
1 quart	Liquid aspic	1 l / 1¾ pints
	Lettuce or other salad greens	
2 - 3	Tomatoes	2 - 3

1. Peel the shallot and chop finely. Melt the butter in a saucepan over a moderate heat, add the shallot and cook until softened.
2. Halve the livers and add to the pan. Cook over a brisk heat

until they are firm and browned but still pink inside.

3. Add salt and pepper to taste. Add a pinch of thyme and the cognac. Remove from the heat and allow to cool completely.

4. Divide the livers between six individual molds and cover with warm aspic. Chill for at least 6 hours or until set.

5. Unmold the livers in aspic onto serving dishes garnished with salad greens and tomato quarters.

Cervelle de canut

Herb-flavored Cheese

	00:15 plus chilling	00:00

American	Ingredients	Metric/Imperial
2	Shallots	2
1 cup	Crème fraîche	250 ml / 8 fl oz
1 lb (2 cups)	Firm cream cheese	500 g / 1 lb
2 tsp	Chopped fresh parsley	2 tsp
1 tbsp	Chopped fresh chives	1 tbsp
3 tbsp	Chopped fresh chervil	3 tbsp
	Salt and pepper	
3 tbsp	Olive oil	3 tbsp
1 tsp	Vinegar	1 tsp

1. Peel and finely chop the shallots.

2. Whisk together the crème fraîche, cream cheese, chopped herbs and shallots. Add salt and pepper to taste. Continuing to stir, incorporate the olive oil and vinegar.

3. Line a round bowl with cheesecloth or muslin. Pour in the cheese mixture, heaping it up well. Fold over the cheesecloth or muslin. Chill for 4 hours.

4. To serve, unwrap the cheese and unmold it onto a serving dish. Serve with raw vegetables or on its own before dessert. The French name for this cheese, which originated in Lyons, means 'silk weaver's brain.'

Fresh peas and parsley (Tomatoes Stuffed with Tuna)

Melons au jambon de Parme

Melon with Parma Ham

	00:05	00:00	
	plus chilling		

American	Ingredients	Metric/Imperial
3	Ripe melons	3
12	Thin slices of parma ham or prosciutto	12
	Pepper	

1. Buy the melons the day before and choose well: they must be very heavy and sweet-smelling. Keep them in the refrigerator overnight.

2. About 30 minutes before serving, cut each melon into quarters and remove the seeds. Remove the peel. Return the melon quarters to the refrigerator to chill for 30 minutes.

3. Wrap each piece of melon in a slice of parma ham and arrange on a long dish. You may add pepper (pepper goes very well with melon).

Melons glacés au porto

Iced Melon with Port Wine

	00:05	00:00	
	plus chilling		

American	Ingredients	Metric/Imperial
3	Ripe melons	3
¾ cup	Port wine	175 ml / 6 fl oz

1. Buy your melons the day before and choose well: they must smell sweet and above all they must be very heavy. Keep them in the refrigerator overnight.

2. About 30 minutes before serving, cut each melon in half and remove the seeds.

3. Pour 2 tablespoons of port wine into each melon half and return to the refrigerator to marinate for 30 minutes.

Pamplemousses grillés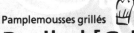

Broiled [Grilled] Grapefruit

	00:02 per fruit	00:05 to 00:08

American	Ingredients	Metric/Imperial
3	Grapefruit	3
	Butter	
6 tbsp	Sugar	6 tbsp

1. Preheat the broiler [grill].
2. Prepare the fruit as in the previous recipe. Place a small pat of butter in the middle of each half and sprinkle with 1 tablespoon of sugar.
3. Arrange the grapefruit halves in a buttered ovenproof dish. Place under the broiler [grill] and cook slowly so that the fruit can be warmed through. Cook until browned on top.
4. Spoon the caramel in the dish over the grapefruit and serve hot, or chill for several hours.

Pamplemousses froids

Chilled Grapefruit

	00:02 per fruit plus chilling	00:00

American	Ingredients	Metric/Imperial
3	Grapefruit	3
1 cup	Sugar	250 g / 8 oz

1. Cut the fruit in half crosswise. Using a very sharp pointed knife, remove the woolly center and the seeds.
2. Separate each section by cutting along the surrounding membrane as far as the peel. Using a serrated grapefruit knife, separate the flesh from the peel.
3. Serve chilled with the sugar.

Pamplemousses cocktail

Grapefruit Cocktail

	00:40 plus chilling	00:00

American	Ingredients	Metric/Imperial
5 - 6	Grapefruit	5 - 6
6	Glacé or maraschino cherries	6
	Sugar	

1. Using a very sharp stainless steel knife, peel the grapefruit without leaving any white pith. Separate the grapefruit into sections, discarding the membrane and seeds. Collect the juice by holding the grapefruit over a bowl as it is prepared.
2. Divide the grapefruit sections and juice between 6 small serving dishes and garnish each with a glacé cherry. Chill until ready to serve.
3. Serve with sugar.

Pommes fourrées au jambon

Apples Stuffed with Ham

| | 00:25 | | 01:00 | |

American	Ingredients	Metric/Imperial
1	Onion	1
¼ cup	Butter	50 g / 2 oz
1	Small sweet red pepper	1
1	Small green pepper	1
5 oz	Cooked ham	150 g / 5 oz
6	Golden Delicious apples	6
2 tbsp	Chopped fresh chives	2 tbsp
6	Black olives	6

1. Preheat the oven to 350°F / 180°C / Gas Mark 4.

2. Peel and chop the onion. Melt the butter in a saucepan and add the chopped onion. Cook until softened without browning.

3. Core and seed the red and green peppers and cut into thin strips. Add to the saucepan and cook until softened. Dice the ham, add to the pan and cook for 5-8 minutes.

4. Cut the tops off the washed apples, and scoop out the insides without piercing the bottom, leaving a shell about ½ in / 1 cm thick.

5. Add the chives to the ham mixture, then use to fill the apples. Arrange in an ovenproof dish and bake for 30-40 minutes.

6. Serve hot, garnished with olives, or cold with salads.

SALADS

The sauce or dressing which binds the ingredients of a salad usually has an oil and vinegar base. According to a Roman saying, four people are needed to make a good salad dressing: a miser to pour the vinegar, a squanderer to add the oil, a wise man for the salt and a madman to stir it.

Céleri en salade

Celery Salad with Roquefort

00:15		00:00

American	Ingredients	Metric/Imperial
2	Heads of celery	2
1 cup	Chopped walnuts	125 g / 4 oz
¼ lb	Roquefort or other blue cheese	125 g / 4 oz
1 tbsp	Cognac	1 tbsp
¼ cup	Walnut oil	4 tbsp
1 tbsp	Wine vinegar	1 tbsp
	Salt and pepper	

1. Trim the celery and remove tough strings, if necessary. Slice finely into a salad bowl. Add the walnuts.
2. Using a fork, crush the cheese and mash in the cognac. Add the oil, vinegar and salt and pepper to taste and mix well.
3. When ready to serve, pour the cheese dressing over the celery. Stir and serve immediately.

Salade de carottes

Carrot Salad

00:20		00:00

American	Ingredients	Metric/Imperial
1½ lb	Carrots	750 g / 1½ lb
	Salt and pepper	
1 tbsp	Vinegar	1 tbsp
1 tbsp	Prepared mustard	1 tbsp
3 tbsp	Oil	3 tbsp
1 tbsp	Chopped fresh chervil or chives	1 tbsp

1. Peel the carrots and grate them.
2. Dissolve a pinch of salt in the vinegar. Mix in the mustard. Add the oil and pepper to taste and mix well.
3. A few minutes before serving, sprinkle the carrots with the dressing and toss well. Sprinkle with the chervil or chives.

Cook's tip: you may replace the vinaigrette dressing with a mixture of crème fraîche and lemon juice.

Chou rouge en salade

Red Cabbage Salad

00:20
plus soaking

00:03

American	Ingredients	Metric/Imperial
1	Head of red cabbage	1
	Salt and pepper	
1¼ cups	Wine vinegar	300 ml / ½ pint
6	Eggs	6
1 cup	Crème fraîche	250 ml / 8 fl oz
1	Lemon	1
1 tbsp	Chopped fresh chervil or parsley	1 tbsp
1 tbsp	Chopped fresh chives	1 tbsp
1 tbsp	Chopped fresh fennel	1 tbsp

1. Remove the coarse and discolored outer leaves from the cabbage. Quarter the cabbage and remove the core. Cut the cabbage into thin strips (julienne).
2. Boil a large quantity of salted water in a saucepan. Add the cabbage. Return to a boil and continue boiling for 2 minutes. Drain the cabbage in a colander, run it under cold water and drain again. Put the cabbage into a mixing bowl and pour over the wine vinegar. Add salt and pepper to taste and leave to marinate for 1 hour, stirring frequently.
3. Hard-cook the eggs for 10 minutes in boiling water. Drain. Remove the shells and crush the eggs with a fork.
4. Mix the eggs with the crème fraîche, the juice of the lemon, the chervil, chives and fennel. Add salt and pepper to taste.
5. Drain the cabbage, discarding the marinade, and place in a salad bowl. Pour the cream sauce over and stir carefully.

Salade composée

Mixed Salad

00:15

00:00

American	Ingredients	Metric/Imperial
1	Head of chicory [curly endive]	1
2	Apples	2
	Lemon juice	
10	Radishes	10
3	Tomatoes	3
1	Head of celery	1
1 cup	Chopped walnuts	125 g / 4 oz
1 tbsp	Prepared mustard with green peppercorns	1 tbsp
¾ cup	Crème fraîche	175 ml / 6 fl oz
2 tbsp	Cider vinegar	2 tbsp
	Salt and pepper	

1. Rinse and drain the chicory. Cut into crosswise shreds with a pair of scissors. Peel and core the apples. Cut into thin slices, sprinkling them with lemon juice as you go to prevent them from discoloring. Trim and slice the radishes. Dice the tomatoes and celery. Place all these ingredients in a salad bowl and scatter over the walnuts.

2. In a mixing bowl, combine the mustard, crème fraîche, vinegar and salt and pepper. Mix well. Serve with the salad.

Salade blanche

White Salad

	00:30 plus chilling	00:50	

American	Ingredients	Metric/Imperial
4	Potatoes	4
2	Apples	2
1	Head of celery	1
1	Fennel bulb	1
⅔ cup	Dry white wine	150 ml / ¼ pint
1 tbsp	Strong prepared mustard	1 tbsp
1½ tbsp	Vinegar	1½ tbsp
4½ tbsp	Oil	4½ tbsp
3 tbsp	Chopped fresh chives or parsley	3 tbsp
	Salt and pepper	
½ cup	Long-grain rice	90 g / 3½ oz
1 quart	Court-bouillon	1 l / 1¾ pints
¾ lb	Cod or other white fish fillet	350 g / 12 oz
1	Head of Romaine [cos] lettuce	1
1 cup	Mayonnaise	250 ml / 8 fl oz
½ cup	Walnuts	50 g / 2 oz
1 cup	Black olives	150 g / 5 oz

1. Place the potatoes in a saucepan and cover with cold water. Bring to a boil and cook for about 20 minutes or until tender. Drain and leave until cool enough to handle.

2. Meanwhile, peel, core and dice the apples. Trim and dice the celery. Cut the fennel into thin strips.

3. Peel and dice the potatoes. Place in a mixing bowl together with the apples, celery and fennel. Add the white wine.

4. Combine the mustard, vinegar, oil and chopped herbs. Season to taste with salt and pepper. Add this dressing to the potato mixture. Toss and chill for 1 hour.

5. Meanwhile, cook the rice in boiling salted water for about 15 minutes or until tender. Drain and add to the potato.

6. Bring the court-bouillon to a simmer in a saucepan. Add the cod and poach for 5 minutes. Remove from the heat and allow the fish to cool in the liquid. Drain the fish and flake into small pieces. Add to the potato mixture.

7. Remove any damaged leaves from the lettuce. Wash in several changes of water and drain. Cut the leaves into strips and use them to line the bottom of a salad bowl.

8. Add half the mayonnaise to the fish salad and fold together gently. Pile on top of the lettuce. Garnish with the walnuts and olives. Serve accompanied by the remainder of the mayonnaise.

Chicorée frisée aux croûtons aillés

Chicory [Endive] with Garlic-Flavored Croûtons

American	Ingredients	Metric/Imperial
00:15		00:05
1	Head of chicory [curly endive]	1
4	Slices of bread	4
7 tbsp	Oil	7 tbsp
2	Garlic cloves	2
	Salt and pepper	
1 tbsp	Vinegar	1 tbsp
1 tbsp	Strong prepared mustard	1 tbsp

1. Remove any damaged leaves from the chicory, rinse carefully and drain in a salad basket.
2. Remove the crust from the slices of bread and dice the bread. Heat 2 tablespoons of the oil in a frying pan and fry the bread dice until golden brown all over. Drain.
3. Peel the garlic, crush finely and mix with 1 tablespoon oil. Add the croûtons to this mixture and stir so that they become saturated.
4. Mix a pinch of salt with the vinegar. Add the mustard and stir thoroughly. Add the remaining oil, pepper to taste and the garlic-flavoured croûtons. Blend. Pour over the chicory [endive] when you are about to serve.

Salade alsacienne

Cheese and Egg Salad

American	Ingredients	Metric/Imperial
00:30		00:10
¾ lb	Emmental cheese	350 g / 12 oz
5	Celery stalks	5
½ lb	Fribourg or other cheese	250 g / 8 oz
1 cup	Walnuts (optional)	125 g / 4 oz
2 tsp	Prepared mustard	2 tsp
2½ - 3 tbsp	Cider vinegar	2½ - 3 tbsp
⅔ cup	Crème fraîche	150 ml / ¼ pint
	Salt and pepper	
3	Eggs	3
1	Bunch of radishes	1

1. Cut the emmental and celery into thin sticks. Dice the fribourg. Put all these ingredients into a salad bowl and mix.
2. In a mixing bowl, mix the mustard with the cider vinegar. Add the crème fraîche gradually, stirring constantly for the

ingredients to blend properly. Add salt and pepper to taste.
3. Hard-cook the eggs for 10 minutes in boiling water. Drain. Remove the shells and cut the eggs in half.
4. Trim and slice the radishes.
5. Put a few spoonfuls of the sauce into the salad bowl and toss well. Garnish with the egg halves and the radishes. Serve the remainder of the sauce separately.

Salade capucine

Marinated Vegetable Salad

	01:00 plus marinating	00:25

American	Ingredients	Metric/Imperial
½ lb	Green beans	250 g / 8 oz
	Salt and pepper	
2 lb	Asparagus	1 kg / 2 lb
1	Cucumber	1
½	Cauliflower	½
1 tbsp	Vinegar	1 tbsp
1 tbsp	Prepared mustard	1 tbsp
3 tbsp	Oil	3 tbsp
1	Medium-size onion	1
1	Bunch of watercress	1
1	Bunch of fresh chervil or parsley	1
2	Fresh tarragon sprigs	2
1	Head of lettuce	1
½	Bunch of radishes	½
1 cup	Mayonnaise	250 ml / 8 fl oz

1. Cut the ends off the green beans and pull to remove any strings. Rinse the beans and cut into pieces. Cook in boiling salted water until crisp-tender. Drain and set aside.
2. Trim the hard ends from the asparagus spears, then scrape the stalks. Cut into pieces about 2 in / 5 cm long. Rinse the asparagus, then cook in boiling salted water for 5-15 minutes (depending on age and size of the spears) or until tender. Drain and set aside.
3. Cut the cucumber into very thin slices. Break the cauliflower into florets.
4. Dissolve a pinch of salt in the vinegar. Mix in the mustard. Add the oil and pepper to taste and mix thoroughly.
5. Peel the onion and chop very finely. Wash the cress leaves, changing the water several times, then chop finely together with the chervil and tarragon. Add the herb mixture and onion to the dressing.
6. Rinse and drain the lettuce, then cut into thin strips. Trim the radishes and slice half of them. Cut the remaining radishes into 'roses'.
7. Put the beans, asparagus, cucumber, cauliflower and sliced radishes into a bowl and sprinkle with the dressing. Mix and leave to marinate for 20-30 minutes.
8. To serve, cover the bottom of a salad bowl with the shredded lettuce and pile the marinated salad on top. Scatter over the radish roses. Serve with the mayonnaise.

Salade d'épinards au lard

Spinach Salad
with Bacon

| | 00:20 | | 00:05 | |

American	Ingredients	Metric/Imperial
½ lb	Smoked bacon	250 g / 8 oz
2	Eggs	2
1 tsp	Strong prepared mustard	1 tsp
1	Lemon	1
	Salt and pepper	
1¼ cups	Olive oil	300 ml / ½ pint
1 lb	Tender young spinach	500 g / 1 lb
1 tbsp	Vegetable oil	1 tbsp
2 tbsp	Wine vinegar	2 tbsp

1. Plunge the bacon into a pan of boiling water and leave to blanch for 5 minutes. Drain, cool and pat dry.

2. Remove any rind and cut the bacon into small pieces.

3. Hard-cook the eggs for 10 minutes in boiling water. Run them under cold water and remove the shells. Separate the yolks from the whites and cut the whites into small cubes. Set the whites aside.

4. Crush the yolks with the mustard and the juice of the lemon until smooth. Add salt and pepper to taste. Incorporate the oil gradually, beating constantly with a wire whisk. Set this mayonnaise aside.

5. Remove the stalks from the spinach and rinse in several changes of water. Drain and pat or shake dry. Place in a salad bowl or on individual plates. Garnish the spinach with the diced egg white.

6. Heat the vegetable oil in a frying pan and add the bacon. Fry until brown and crisp. Drain the bacon on paper towels, then scatter over the spinach.

7. Pour away the oil from the frying pan. Add the vinegar to the pan and stir to mix with the sediment. Boil for a few seconds, then pour over the spinach.

8. Serve accompanied by the mayonnaise.

Salade de flageolets

Bean Salad

| | 00:15 | 01:30 |

American	Ingredients	Metric/Imperial
2 cups (1 lb)	Dried or fresh flageolet beans	500 g / 1 lb
1	Onion	1
1	Clove	1
1	Garlic clove	1
1	Carrot	1
1	Bouquet garni	1
1	Knackwurst, saveloy or other large cooked pork sausage	1
	Salt and pepper	
1 tbsp	Wine vinegar	1 tbsp
1 tbsp	Prepared mustard	1 tbsp
3 tbsp	Oil	3 tbsp
	Chopped fresh herbs (parsley, chives, etc)	

1. Place the dried beans in a large saucepan containing at least 3 quarts [3 l / 5 pints] water and add the peeled onion studded with the clove, the peeled garlic, peeled carrot and bouquet garni. Bring slowly to a boil and leave to cook for at least 1½ hours. (Cook fresh beans briefly until just tender.)
2. Meanwhile, heat the sausage: toss it into a saucepan of boiling water, remove from the heat and allow the sausage to warm through for 10 minutes. Drain the sausage, skin it and cut into slices. Set aside.
3. Drain the beans and place in a mixing bowl.
4. Dissolve a pinch of salt in the vinegar. Mix in the mustard. Add the oil, pepper to taste and chopped herbs. Mix thoroughly.
5. Pour the dressing over the still warm beans and toss to coat. Spoon into a salad bowl, top with the sausage slices and serve.

Laitue de Trévise

Radicchio Salad

| | 00:10 | 00:00 |

American	Ingredients	Metric/Imperial
1 lb	Radicchio or red chicory	500 g / 1 lb
	Salt and pepper	
1 tbsp	Vinegar	1 tbsp
¼ cup	Oil	4 tbsp
2	Anchovy fillets	2
½	Garlic clove	½

1. Remove the damaged leaves from the radicchio, rinse carefully and drain thoroughly in a salad basket.
2. Mix a pinch of salt with the vinegar. Add the oil, crushed anchovy fillets, peeled and crushed garlic and pepper to taste. Stir and pour over the radicchio when you are about to serve.

Poivrons grillés en salade

Broiled [Grilled] Pepper Salad

	00:30 plus marinating		00:15
American	**Ingredients**	**Metric/Imperial**	
2 lb	Sweet red peppers	1 kg / 2 lb	
1	Garlic clove	1	
1 ¼ cups	Olive oil	300 ml / ½ pint	
	Salt and pepper		

1. Preheat the broiler [grill].
2. Halve the peppers and place them cut sides down under the broiler. Cook until the skins are charred and blistered.
3. Wrap the peppers in paper and allow to cool for 10 minutes. Remove them from the paper and peel off the skins.
4. Remove the core and seeds from the peppers and cut them into strips. Peel and finely chop the garlic and sprinkle over the peppers. Cover with oil. Add salt and pepper to taste. Leave to marinate for at least 24 hours.
5. Serve as an hors d'oeuvre or condiment.

Salade montmartroise

Chicory [Endive], Bacon and Gruyère Salad

	00:15		00:05
American	**Ingredients**	**Metric/Imperial**	
½ lb	Smoked bacon	250 g / 8 oz	
½	Loaf of french bread	½	
3 - 4	Garlic cloves	3 - 4	
5 oz	Gruyère cheese	150 g / 5 oz	
1	Head of chicory [curly endive]	1	
	Salt and pepper		
1 tbsp	Vinegar	1 tbsp	
1 tsp	Prepared mustard	1 tsp	
¼ cup	Oil	4 tbsp	

1. Cut the bacon into chunks and blanch in boiling water for 5 minutes. Drain and allow to cool, then cook in a frying pan until browned and crisp. Drain and keep warm.
2. Cut the french loaf into thin slices. Toast them, then rub on both sides with the cut sides of the halved garlic cloves.
3. Cut the gruyère into ¾ in / 2 cm cubes.
4. Rinse the chicory, drain and tear into small pieces. Place in a salad bowl.
5. Dissolve a pinch of salt in the vinegar. Add the mustard and mix, then stir in the oil and pepper to taste.
6. Add the dressing to the chicory and toss. Scatter over the bacon and cheese cubes. Serve the toast separately.

Endives, pommes, raisins de Smyrne

Endive [Chicory] with Apples

	00:15	00:00
American	**Ingredients**	**Metric/Imperial**
½ cup	Golden raisins [sultanas]	75 g / 3 oz
4	Heads of Belgian endive [chicory]	4
2	Apples	2
	Lemon juice	
	Salt and pepper	
1 tbsp	Vinegar	1 tbsp
1 tbsp	Strong prepared mustard	1 tbsp
3 tbsp	Oil	3 tbsp

1. Soak the raisins in warm water for 30 minutes.
2. Remove any damaged leaves from the endive. Cut into slices crosswise. Core and dice the unpeeled apples. Sprinkle with lemon juice to prevent them discoloring.
3. Dissolve a pinch of salt in the vinegar. Mix in the mustard. Add the oil and pepper to taste and blend.
4. Drain the raisins and combine with the endive and apples in a salad bowl. Pour over the dressing, mix and serve.

Belgian endive (chicory)

Scarole, noix, truffe

Walnut and Truffle Salad

	00:15	00:00
American	**Ingredients**	**Metric/Imperial**
1	Head of escarole	1
1	Truffle	1
1 cup	Chopped walnuts	125 g / 4 oz
	Salt and pepper	
2 tbsp	Sherry vinegar	2 tbsp
¼ cup	Walnut or peanut oil	4 tbsp

1. Remove any damaged leaves from the escarole, rinse and drain in a salad basket. Peel the truffle and cut into thin sticks. Combine the escarole, truffle and walnuts in a salad bowl.
2. Dissolve a pinch of salt in the vinegar. Add the oil and pepper to taste. Blend and pour over the salad. Toss and serve.

Salade Côte d'Ivoire

Ivory Coast Salad

| | 01:00 plus chilling | | 00:20 | |

American	Ingredients	Metric/Imperial
6	Large raw shrimp [prawns]	6
	Salt and pepper	
3	Whiting fillets	3
2	Grapefruit	2
1	Small ripe pineapple	1
3	Papayas	3
2	Avocados	2
	Lemon juice	
1	Egg yolk	1
1½ tsp	Strong prepared mustard	1½ tsp
	Tabasco sauce	
1 cup	Oil	250 ml / 8 fl oz
1 tsp	Wine vinegar	1 tsp

1. Cook the shrimp in boiling salted water until the shells turn pink. Remove with a slotted spoon and leave to cool.
2. Add the whiting fillets to the shrimp cooking water. As soon as the water returns to a boil, remove the saucepan from the heat and leave the fillets in the water for 5-7 minutes. Drain and carefully pat dry with paper towels. Cut the whiting fillets into pieces.
3. Peel the grapefruit. Divide into sections, removing all seeds and membrane. Catch the juice from the grapefruit in a bowl.
4. Peel the pineapple and cut into small pieces.
5. Cut the papayas in half lengthwise. Remove the seeds and a little of the surrounding flesh with a spoon, leaving shells about ½ in / 1 cm thick. Chop the removed flesh, and set the shells aside.
6. Peel the avocados and remove the seeds. Dice the flesh. Sprinkle immediately with lemon juice to prevent them from turning black.
7. Put the whiting, avocados, grapefruit sections, pineapple and chopped papaya flesh in a bowl and mix together. Divide between the papaya shells.
8. Put the egg yolk into a bowl and add the mustard and tabasco, salt and pepper to taste. Whisk to mix, then gradually add the oil in a thin trickle, whisking continuously. Thin out the mayonnaise with the vinegar. Lighten it with the reserved grapefruit juice.
9. Spoon some of the mayonnaise over the stuffed papaya halves and place the remainder in a sauceboat. Garnish each half with a peeled and deveined shrimp. Serve the salad lightly chilled.

Salade de pissenlits au lard

Dandelion Salad with Bacon

	00:15	00:05 to 00:07

American	Ingredients	Metric/Imperial
¾ lb	Lightly salted or smoked bacon	350 g / 12 oz
1 ½ lb	Dandelion leaves	750 g / 1 ½ lb
	Salt and pepper	
1 tbsp	Vinegar	1 tbsp
1 tsp	Prepared mustard	1 tsp
3 tbsp	Oil	3 tbsp

1. If the bacon is salty, put it into a saucepan of cold water, bring to a boil and blanch for 5 minutes. Drain, cool and pat dry.
2. Rinse the dandelion leaves in several changes of water and shake dry. Place in a salad bowl.
3. Dissolve a pinch of salt in the vinegar. Add the mustard, oil and pepper to taste. Pour over the drained dandelion leaves.
4. Cut the bacon into pieces as thick or as thin as you like. Cook in a frying pan, without fat, until crisp and well browned. Pour the bacon over the dandelion leaves together with the bacon fat in the pan. Take immediately to the table, toss and serve.

Salade à la tapenade

Piquant Olive Salad

	00:25	00:20

American	Ingredients	Metric/Imperial
1 lb	Small potatoes	500 g / 1 lb
1 lb	Small tomatoes	500 g / 1 lb
½ lb	Small onions	250 g / 8 oz
1	Garlic clove	1
2 tbsp	Olive, anchovy and caper spread	2 tbsp
6 tbsp	Olive oil	6 tbsp
1 tbsp	Vinegar	1 tbsp
2 tbsp	Chopped fresh parsley	2 tbsp
	Salt and pepper	
1 cup	Black olives	150 g / 5 oz

1. Put the unpeeled potatoes in a saucepan of cold water. Bring to a boil and cook for 20 minutes. Drain and leave to cool, then peel and quarter.
2. Quarter the tomatoes.
3. Peel and thinly slice the onions. Peel and crush the garlic.
4. Mix the olive, anchovy and caper spread in a bowl with the olive oil, garlic, vinegar and chopped parsley. Taste, then add salt and pepper.
5. Put the potatoes, tomatoes and onions in a salad bowl. Add the dressing and olives, toss and serve.

Salade de tomates

Tomato Salad

🔪 00:10		00:00 🥘
American	**Ingredients**	**Metric/Imperial**
3	Scallions [spring onions]	3
8	Small, very firm tomatoes	8
1 cup	Small black olives	125 g / 4 oz
	Salt and pepper	
1 tbsp	Vinegar	1 tbsp
1 tsp	Prepared mustard	1 tsp
3 tbsp	Oil	3 tbsp

1. Trim and chop the scallions and place in a salad bowl. Cut each tomato into 4 slices and place on the scallions together with the olives.
2. Dissolve a pinch of salt in the vinegar. Mix in the mustard. Add the oil and pepper to taste and mix well.
3. Add the dressing to the tomatoes and serve.

Salade de crabes à la languedocienne

Languedoc Crab Salad

🔪 00:20 plus chilling		01:10 🥘
American	**Ingredients**	**Metric/Imperial**
4	Carrots	4
2	Garlic cloves	2
4	Onions	4
1	Fresh thyme sprig	1
1	Bay leaf	1
2 quarts	Water	2 l / 3½ pints
1¼ cups + 3 tbsp	Vinegar	300 ml / ½ pint + 3 tbsp
	Salt and pepper	
2 (1 lb)	Crabs	2 (500 g / 1 lb)
2	Eggs	2
1 tsp	Prepared mustard	1 tsp
5 tbsp	Oil	5 tbsp

1. Peel and slice the carrots, garlic and onions. Place in a large saucepan together with the thyme, bay leaf, water, 1¼ cups [300 ml / ½ pint] vinegar, and salt and pepper to taste. Bring to a boil and simmer for 40 minutes.
2. Place the crabs in the simmering court-bouillon. Cook for 15 minutes.
3. Meanwhile, hard-cook the eggs for 10 minutes in boiling water. Drain and cool.
4. When the crabs are cooked, drain them. Detach the claws and legs, remove the flesh and cut into small pieces. Open the shell. Discard all inedible parts, then remove the creamy parts and the flesh and cut into small cubes.
5. Shell the eggs and cut in half. Cut the whites into thin strips and crush the yolks with a fork.
6. In a mixing bowl, mix the creamy parts of the crabs with the

egg yolks until smooth. Add salt and pepper to taste, the mustard, the remaining vinegar and the oil, stirring well. Add the crabmeat to this dressing and toss to coat.

7. Place in a salad bowl. Scatter over the strips of egg white and chill for 1 hour before serving.

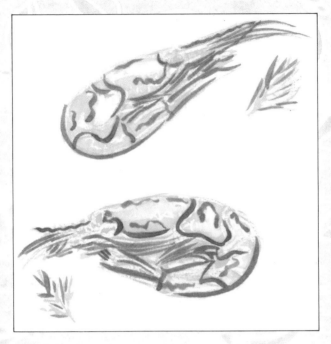

Salade de langoustines

Shrimp [Prawn] Salad

🔪	00:20 plus marinating		00:10 🍲
American	**Ingredients**		**Metric/Imperial**
2 tbsp	Golden raisins [sultanas]		2 tbsp
	Salt and pepper		
12	Raw jumbo shrimp [Dublin Bay prawns]		12
1	Head of celery		1
2	Apples		2
1 tbsp	Vinegar		1 tbsp
1 tbsp	Strong prepared mustard		1 tbsp
3 tbsp	Oil		3 tbsp
2 tbsp	Mayonnaise		2 tbsp

1. Put the raisins to soak in warm water.

2. Bring a large saucepan of salted water to a boil. Add the shrimp. When the water returns to a boil, cook for 6 minutes.

3. Drain the shrimp and cool in cold water. Peel and devein them and cut in half lengthwise.

4. Trim and dice the celery. Peel, core and dice the apples.

5. In a salad bowl, combine the shrimp, celery, apples and drained raisins.

6. Dissolve a pinch of salt in the vinegar. Mix in the mustard. Add the oil and pepper to taste. Stir in the mayonnaise.

7. Pour the dressing into the salad bowl and stir to mix. Leave to marinate for 10 minutes.

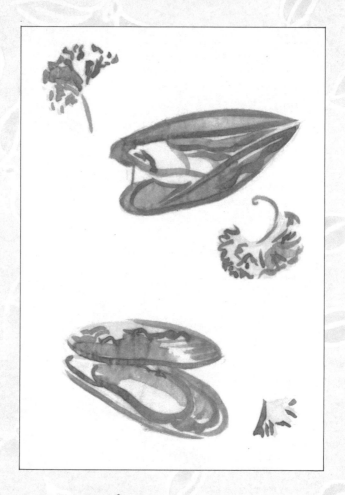

Salade napolitaine

Neapolitan Seafood Salad

American	Ingredients	Metric/Imperial
	🔪 00:30 plus marinating	00:30 🍲
1 lb	Squid	500 g / 1 lb
	Court-bouillon	
1 quart	Clams or cockles	750 g / 1½ lb
⅔ cup	Dry white wine	150 ml / ¼ pint
1 quart	Mussels	750 g / 1½ lb
1¼ cups	Olive oil	300 ml / ½ pint
½	Lemon	½
	Chopped fresh chives and parsley	
	Salt and pepper	
3	Tomatoes	3
	Salad greens	

1. Buy the squid already cleaned. Cut the triangular bodies into thin strips. Place these and the tentacles (if available) in a saucepan and cover with court-bouillon. Bring to a boil and simmer for 7-10 minutes. Do not overcook or the squid will be tough. Remove from the heat and leave to cool in the liquid. Drain.

2. Scrub the clams or cockles and place them in a large saucepan with the wine. Cook over a brisk heat, shaking the pan frequently, until they open. (Discard any that remain closed.) Take them out of their shells. Strain the cooking liquid through cheesecloth or muslin, or use a coffee filter. Set the liquid aside.

3. Scrub the mussels and place them in a stewpan over a brisk heat. Cook until they open, and remove them from their shells. (Discard any that remain closed.)

4. Combine two-thirds of the clam cooking liquid, the olive oil, lemon juice, herbs, and salt and pepper to taste. Mix well. Add the squid, clams or cockles and mussels and leave to marinate for 25-30 minutes, stirring occasionally.

5. Quarter the tomatoes.

6. Shred the salad greens and place over the bottom of a salad bowl. Pour in the seafood salad and garnish with the tomato quarters.

Salade aux noisettes

Hazelnut Salad

00:40   00:00

American	Ingredients	Metric/Imperial
1	Head of celeriac	1
	Lemon juice	
4	Carrots	4
1	Small head of celery	1
4	Tomatoes	4
1	Bunch of radishes	1
1	Head of escarole	1
2	Thick slices of cooked ham	2
½ cup	Hazelnuts	50 g / 2 oz
5 tbsp	Vegetable oil	5 tbsp
3 tbsp	Dry sherry wine	3 tbsp
1½ tsp	Wine vinegar	1½ tsp
1 tsp	Prepared mustard with herbs	1 tsp
	Salt and pepper	
12	Black olives	12

1. Peel the celeriac, grate it and sprinkle with a few drops of lemon juice to prevent it from discoloring.

2. Peel the carrots and grate them. Dice the celery. Quarter the tomatoes. Slice the radishes. Remove the damaged leaves from the escarole, rinse carefully and tear into small pieces. Cut the ham into thin strips. Crush the hazelnuts coarsely.

3. Put the celeriac, carrots, celery, tomatoes, radishes, escarole and ham into a salad bowl.

4. In a bowl mix together the oil, sherry, wine vinegar, mustard with herbs and the crushed hazelnuts. Add salt and pepper to taste and leave for a few minutes so the flavors can intermingle.

5. Pour the dressing over the salad. Add the olives, stir and serve.

TERRINES, PÂTÉS and GALANTINES

Do you know the difference between a pâté and a terrine? The word pâté is used for all sorts of preparations based on meat or fish, covered with pastry and baked in the oven.

On the other hand, terrines are cooked in fireproof earthenware or china, stoneware, enameled iron, or glass containers. In everyday speech, terrines and pâtés are often confused. Many 'pâtés' are cooked in terrines.

Galantines, however, consist of chopped meat or fish rolled up in the animal's skin, then cooked in bouillon in a saucepan. The word 'galantine' is said to come from the words *geline* or *galine,* the Old French for 'chicken,' since this dish was at first made of poultry, and then later, at the end of the seventeenth century, of game and meat.

There are many varieties of pâté. Each region of France has its own recipe for pâtés, terrines and galantines. We have only selected a few simple ones for this chapter.

Guidelines

The ingredients
The ingredients used to make the filling can be many and varied: pork, mixtures of pork and veal, poultry and game (hare, duck, young wild boar, pheasant, quail, etc), foie gras, usually covered with a thin caul of pork and placed whole in the middle of the filling, panadas (a mixture of bread soaked in milk, flour, water, butter and egg, which is for binding light fillings such as fish or shellfish fillings), truffles, which give the filling their very characteristic flavor and note of refinement, and alcohols such as brandy, armagnac or calvados and white wine, madeira, port and sherry.

Lastly, the seasoning: only if none of the ingredients of the filling has been already salted, add salt.

Equipment
A meat grinder [mincer] or food processor is essential to grind the ingredients quickly and cleanly. It replaces our grandmothers' heavy mortar and pestle.

Cooking terrines and pâtés
The inside of a terrine must be lined with fat for the cooking process. The filling should also be covered with fat. A bay leaf and some sprigs of thyme are placed on top, and flavor the terrine by being concentrated under the lid during the cooking process. The terrine is next placed in a shallow baking pan, and surrounded by hot (but not boiling) water up to one-third of its height. Using a water bath or prevents the filling from drying out.

Checking the cooking process
You can usually expect the cooking to take about 1½ hours, but the time actually depends on the composition of the terrine or pâté. Check the fat surrounding the terrine. As soon as it

becomes very clear, the terrine is cooked.

After cooking
The terrine must cool for 1 hour. The filling is then compressed by putting a board on it, on top of which is placed a weight, and the terrine is kept overnight in the refrigerator. It will keep for a week.

Cooking galantines
These are cooked slowly for about 1½ hours. The water or broth must be just barely simmering. The best way to check the temperature is to put a cooking thermometer in the liquid. To ensure that the galantine keeps its cylindrical shape during cooking, wrap it in cheesecloth or muslin.

Terrine de foie gras

Foie Gras Terrine

	00:20 plus chilling		00:30

American	Ingredients	Metric/Imperial
1 (1½ lb)	Goose liver	1 (750 g / 1½ lb)
2 tbsp	Coarse salt	2 tbsp
½ tsp	Dried fennel	½ tsp
	Pepper	
3 tbsp	Armagnac	3 tbsp
2 tsp	Unflavored gelatin	2 tsp
1½ cups	Port wine	350 ml / 12 fl oz
1	Piece of pork caul without holes	1

1. Remove the skin from the goose liver, then take out all the tubes. Sprinkle with coarse salt and chill for at least 24 hours in the refrigerator.
2. Rinse the liver in cold water to clean off the salt and pat dry. Put the liver in a bowl, season with the fennel and pepper to taste and rub in with your fingers. Add the armagnac. Dissolve the gelatin in 2 tablespoons of the port and add to the bowl. Chill for 48 hours.
3. Soak the caul in cold water.
4. Preheat the oven to 400°F / 200°C / Gas Mark 6.
5. Drain the caul and lay it out on a cloth. Pat dry. Wrap the liver in the caul and place in a small casserole. Add the remaining port, which should cover the liver. Cover the casserole.
6. Place in the oven. When the port starts to simmer, cook for a further 10 minutes.
7. Take the casserole out of the oven and allow to cool slightly, then drain the liver and put it into a small terrine. Reserve the liquid in the casserole. Cover the liver with a board, put a weight on top and leave to cool for 12 hours. Also allow the cooking liquid to cool.
8. Remove the fat from the cooled cooking liquid and pour it over the liver. Chill for at least 24 hours longer.

Galantine

Galantine

	01:00		01:30	
	plus cooking and chilling		Serves 8	

American	Ingredients	Metric/Imperial
1 (3½ lb)	Chicken	1 (1.5 kg / 3½ lb)
	Salt and pepper	
½ lb	Boneless pork shoulder	250 g / 8 oz
½ lb	Boneless veal shoulder	250 g / 8 oz
¼ lb	Veal kidney fat	125 g / 4 oz
¾ cup	Soft bread crumbs	40 g / 1½ oz
⅔ cup	Milk	150 ml / ¼ pint
3	Shallots	3
2	Onions	2
2 tbsp	Chopped fresh herbs (tarragon, parsley and chives)	2 tbsp
2	Eggs	2
2	Fresh thyme sprigs	2
	Grated nutmeg	
2	Chicken livers	2
2 quarts	Water	2 l / 3½ pints
1	Chicken bouillon [stock] cube	1
1 envelope	Unflavored gelatin	1 tbsp

1. Have the butcher or poulterer prepare the chicken if possible: remove the skin from the chicken, with the meat adhering to it, cut the wing and thigh joints, and remove and discard the carcass.

2. Spread out the skin. Cut away the area in front of the thighs, and sew up the tail opening with kitchen string. Season with salt and pepper to taste.

3. Finely grind (mince) all the chicken meat, including the breast fillets. Also grind the pork, veal and kidney fat. Mix these together in a bowl.

4. Moisten the breadcrumbs with the milk and squeeze out the excess. Peel and chop the shallots and onions. Add the breadcrumbs, shallots and onions to the meat mixture. Add the chopped herbs, eggs, crumbled thyme, a pinch of grated nutmeg and salt and pepper to taste. Mix the ingredients for the filling thoroughly.

5. Arrange half the filling on the chicken skin. Place the chicken livers on top, and cover with the rest of the filling. Fold over the edges of the skin and sew it up with kitchen string. Wrap the whole thing in cheesecloth or muslin and tie it up with string.

6. Bring the water to a boil in a saucepan and dissolve the bouillon cube in it. Put the galantine in the saucepan and bring back to a boil over a high heat. Reduce the heat and leave to simmer gently for 1½ hours. Remove from the heat and leave the galantine to cool in the stock.

7. Take the galantine out of the stock, unwrap it, and leave to become completely cold. Boil the stock until reduced to 2 cups (500 ml/¾ pint).

8. Dissolve the gelatin according to package directions, then add to the stock. Allow this aspic to cool until lukewarm.

9. Coat the galatine with the warm, jellying aspic and chill until set.

Pâté chaud paysan

Hot Country Pâté

	00:20		01:00	
	plus marinating, and thawing or making pastry			

American	Ingredients	Metric/Imperial
1 lb	Boneless pork shoulder	500 g / 1 lb
1 lb	Boneless veal shoulder	500 g / 1 lb
⅔ cup	Riesling or other white wine	150 ml / ¼ pint
1	Bay leaf	1
1	Fresh thyme sprig	1
1	Clove	1
	Chopped fresh parsley	
	Grated nutmeg	
	Salt and pepper	
2 tbsp	Oil	2 tbsp
¼ lb	Puff pastry	125 g / 4 oz
½ quantity	Basic short pastry	½ quantity
1	Egg yolk	1

1. Cut the pork and veal into thin slices. Put into a mixing bowl with the wine, crumbled bay leaf and thyme, crushed clove, chopped parsley, a pinch of grated nutmeg, and salt and pepper to taste. Add the oil and stir to mix. Leave to marinate in a cool place for 12 hours.

2. The next day, preheat to 425°F / 220°C / Gas Mark 7. Thaw the puff pastry if using frozen.

3. Roll out the basic short pastry on a lightly floured surface and cut into an 8×6 in / 20×15 cm strip. Use to line the bottom and sides of a terrine or loaf pan.

4. Pour the marinated meat mixture into the terrine.

5. Roll out the puff pastry and use to cover the meat filling. Press the edges of the pastries together to seal. Brush the surface with egg yolk. Make a small hole in the center and insert a piece of rolled-up cardboard as a 'chimney' or use a pie funnel.

6. Bake for 15 minutes, then reduce the temperature to 350°F / 180°C / Gas Mark 4 and bake for 45 minutes longer. Serve hot.

Nutmeg and thyme

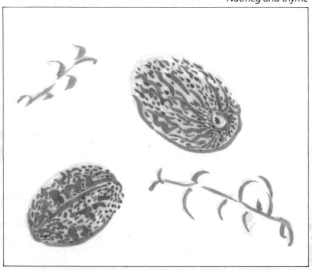

Pâté de foie de porc

Pork Liver Pâté

| | 00:50 *plus cooling* | | 03:00 | |

American	Ingredients	Metric/Imperial
3	Carrots	3
3	Turnips	3
4	Onions	4
3	Cloves	3
3	Leeks	3
2 lb	Pork bones	1 kg / 2 lb
1	Piece of bacon rind	1
1	Bouquet garni	1
	Salt and pepper	
3 quarts	Water	3 l / 5 pints
¼ lb	Fatty bacon	125 g / 4 oz
1 lb	Fresh pork sides [belly pork]	500 g / 1 lb
1	Bunch of fresh parsley	1
1	Large piece of pork caul	1
1 lb	Pork liver	500 g / 1 lb
2 tbsp	Brandy	2 tbsp
	Cayenne pepper	
	Grated nutmeg	
1	Bay leaf	1

1. Peel the carrots and turnips. Peel 1 onion and stud it with 2 of the cloves. Put these vegetables in a saucepan, together with the leeks, bones, bacon rind, bouquet garni, and salt and pepper to taste. Cover with the water, bring to a boil and simmer gently for 1½ hours.

2. Meanwhile, peel and chop the remaining onions. Grind the remaining clove to a powder. Finely grind (mince) the bacon and pork sides. Chop the parsley. Put the caul to soak in cold water.

3. Preheat the oven to 400°F/200°C/Gas Mark 6.

4. After the stock has simmered for 1½ hours, add the pork liver and continue to simmer for 8-10 minutes. Remove the liver from the stock, allow it to drain, then leave it to cool before grinding (mincing) finely.

5. In a bowl, mix together the liver, bacon, pork, parsley and onions. Add the brandy, and season to taste with salt, freshly ground black pepper, cayenne pepper and a pinch of grated nutmeg. Add the ground clove, and mix all these ingredients together thoroughly.

6. Carefully drain the caul and lay it out on a cloth. Pat it dry. Arrange it in a 1½ quart [1.5 1/2½ pint] terrine, leaving it hanging over the sides. Put the bay leaf on the bottom, and fill the terrine with the liver mixture, heaping it up well. Fold the caul over the top.

7. Put the lid on the terrine and put it in a baking pan containing 2 in/5 cm water. Put both in the oven and cook for 1¼ hours. The water must just simmer.

8. Remove the terrine from the oven. Take off the lid, put a board and then a weight on top of the pâté and leave to cool. Then place in the refrigerator and chill for several hours or overnight before serving.

Pâté de foies de volaille

Chicken Liver Pâté

	00:30 plus chilling		00:35

American	Ingredients	Metric/Imperial
¾ lb	Onions	350 g / 12 oz
¼ cup	Goose fat or butter	4 tbsp
1¼ lb	Chicken livers	625 g / 1¼ lb
2 tsp	Dried thyme	2 tsp
	Salt and pepper	

1. Peel and chop the onions. Heat 2 tablespoons of the goose fat or butter in a frying pan, add the onions and cook until softened. Remove the onions and put to one side.

2. Put the rest of the goose fat or butter in the frying pan. Add the livers and cook for 5-7 minutes, stirring frequently. Add the thyme, mix together and allow to cool.

3. Put the livers and onions in a blender or food processor, or through a food mill, to obtain a very smooth purée. If necessary, put the mixture through twice. Season to taste with salt and pepper and mix thoroughly. Spoon the mixture into a 1½ quart [1.5 l / 2½ pint] terrine. Chill for several hours.

4. This pâté will keep perfectly for 8-10 days in the refrigerator. Ensure that the terrine is covered, so that it does not dry.

Lapin en gelée

Rabbit in Wine Aspic

	00:30 plus marinating		02:00

American	Ingredients	Metric/Imperial
1 (3½ - 4 lb)	Rabbit	1 (1.5 - 1.8 kg / 3½ - 4 lb)
6	White onions	6
2	Fresh thyme sprigs	2
1	Bunch of fresh parsley	1
6	Slices of smoked pork tenderloin [fillet]	6
	Salt and pepper	
2 cups	Dry white wine	500 ml / ¾ pint

1. Using a sharp knife, cut the rabbit into pieces.

2. Peel and chop the onions. Crumble the thyme. Chop the parsley. Mix all 3 ingredients together.

3. Line the bottom of a terrine with 4 slices of smoked pork. Cover with a layer of rabbit pieces, lightly season with salt and pepper, and sprinkle with the herb mixture. Add more rabbit pieces, salt, pepper and herbs. Finish with rabbit pieces, and cover with the last 2 slices of pork. Add half the dry white wine, and leave to marinate, without a lid, in a cool place for 5 hours.

4. Preheat the oven to 350°F / 180°C / Gas Mark 4.

5. Put the lid on the terrine, place it in the oven and cook for 30 minutes. Check to be sure the juice is not bubbling up over the sides. Leave to cook for a further 1½ hours, adding the rest of the white wine a little at a time.

6. Take the terrine out of the oven. Place a board on the meat, add a weight on top, and leave to cool completely. The terrine should keep for more than a week in the refrigerator.

HOT
HORS D'OEUVRES

Corniottes

Cream Cheese Pastries

🔪	00:30 plus making pastry		00:30 🍳
American	**Ingredients**		**Metric/Imperial**
1 quantity	Basic short pastry		1 quantity
4	Eggs		4
5 oz	Cream cheese		150 g / 5 oz
5 tbsp	Crème fraîche		5 tbsp
	Salt and pepper		

1. Preheat the oven to 450°F / 230°C / Gas Mark 8.
2. Roll out the pastry and cut out 4 in / 10 cm diameter rounds. Raise the edges of the rounds to form little tricorns, pinching them at the corners.
3. Break the eggs into a mixing bowl and beat to mix. Add the cream cheese, crème fraîche, and salt and pepper to taste, and work to obtain a smooth mixture.
4. Fill each tricorn with the cheese mixture. Place them on a baking sheet or in tartlet molds, if you think that the mixture will overflow.
5. Bake for 30 minutes.

Barquettes chaudes au cantal

Hot Pastry Boats with Cheese

🔪	00:10 plus making pastry boats		00:10 🍳
American	**Ingredients**		**Metric/Imperial**
2 cups	Grated cantal or similar cheese		250 g / 8 oz
5 tbsp	Crème fraîche		5 tbsp
	Pepper		
1 tsp	Butter		1 tsp
⅓ cup	Chopped smoked lean bacon		60 g / 2½ oz
6	Baked pastry boats		6

1. Preheat the oven to 400°F / 200°C / Gas Mark 6.
2. Combine the cheese, crème fraîche and pepper to taste in a mixing bowl.
3. Melt the butter in a frying pan, add the bacon and fry until browned. Drain on paper towels.
4. Put the pieces of bacon into the pastry boats and cover with the cheese mixture. Bake for 5-7 minutes. Serve very hot.

Brioche

Brioches chaudes fromage-chipolatas

Hot Cheese and Sausage Brioches

	00:20		00:20	

American	Ingredients	Metric/Imperial
6	Small individual brioches	6
3	Small pork link sausages [chipolatas]	3
2½ tbsp	Butter	30 g / 1¼ oz
2½ tbsp	Flour	30 g / 1¼ oz
1¾ cups	Milk	450 ml / ¾ pint
	Grated nutmeg	
	Salt and pepper	
1¼ cups	Grated gruyère cheese	150 g / 5 oz

1. Preheat the oven to 425°F / 220°C / Gas Mark 7.
2. Remove the tops of the brioches and scoop out the soft insides using a small spoon. Do not break the crust.
3. Pierce the sausages with a fork, place them in a frying pan without fat and brown them gently all over. Drain and cut into small cubes.
4. Melt the butter in a saucepan over a gentle heat, stir in the flour and cook for 1 minute. Gradually mix in the milk using a wire whisk. Cook, stirring, until the sauce is thick. Add a pinch of nutmeg, and salt and pepper to taste. Add the gruyère and sausage pieces and stir to mix.
5. Stuff the brioches with this preparation, put their tops back on and put them into an ovenproof dish. Heat for 5 minutes in the oven and serve immediately.

49

Barquettes chaudes aux fines herbes

Hot Pastry Boats with Herbs

	00:10		00:06	
	plus making pastry boats			

American	Ingredients	Metric/Imperial
6	Baked pastry boats	6
1	Small bunch of fresh herbs (tarragon, parsley, chives)	1
3	Eggs	3
¼ cup	Crème fraîche	4 tbsp
	Salt and pepper	

1. Preheat the oven to 325°F / 160°C / Gas Mark 3.
2. Arrange the pastry boats on a baking sheet and put them into the oven to heat through.
3. Meanwhile, finely chop the herbs. Break the eggs into a bowl and add the crème fraîche and salt and pepper to taste. Put this bowl into a saucepan half full of hot water and cook over a medium heat for about 5 minutes, stirring continuously. When the mixture is thick and very smooth, blend in the chopped herbs.
4. Fill the hot pastry boats with the herb mixture and serve immediately.

Gougère

Cheese Pastry Ring

	00:20		00:40	

American	Ingredients	Metric/Imperial
1½ oz	Gruyère cheese	40 g / 1½ oz
1 cup	Water	250 ml / 8 fl oz
	Salt and pepper	
5 tbsp	Butter	65 g / 2½ oz
1 cup	Flour	125 g / 4 oz
4	Eggs	4
1¼ cups	Grated gruyère cheese	150 g λ5 oz
1	Egg yolk	1

1. Preheat the oven to 350°F / 180°C / Gas Mark 4. Cut the piece of gruyère into thin slices.
2. Bring the water to a boil in a saucepan together with a pinch of salt and the butter. Add the flour all at once. Mix vigorously with a wooden spoon until the dough comes away from the sides of the pan. Remove the saucepan from the heat. Add one whole egg and mix thoroughly, then add another whole egg and mix. Continue adding the remaining whole eggs, incorporating each thoroughly before adding the next. Add a pinch of pepper, ¾ cup [75 g / 3 oz] of the grated cheese and the slices of gruyère.
3. Butter and flour a baking sheet. Spoon the dough onto it in a ring. Brush with the beaten egg yolk and sprinkle with the rest of the grated gruyère.
4. Bake for about 40 minutes.

Chavignols grillés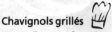

Baked Goat's Cheese

🔪 00:15 00:12 to 00:13 🍲

American	Ingredients	Metric/Imperial
	Salt and pepper	
1 tbsp	Vinegar	1 tbsp
3 tbsp	Walnut oil	3 tbsp
15	Walnuts	15
1	Head of chicory [curly endive]	1
6	Crottin de Chavignol or similar small, soft goat's cheese	6
6	Slices of bread	6

1. Preheat the oven to 425°F / 220°C / Gas Mark 7.
2. Dissolve a pinch of salt in the vinegar. Add the oil, walnuts and pepper to taste. Place in the bottom of a salad bowl and set aside.
3. Rinse and drain the chicory. Separate the leaves. Add to the salad bowl but do not toss.
4. Cut a ½ in / 1 cm slice from the base of each cheese. Reserve these slices for another recipe. Cut the cheeses in half.
5. Trim the slices of bread so they are just slightly larger than the cheeses. Place a halved cheese on each slice of bread.
6. Arrange the toasts on a baking sheet and bake for 8 minutes. Then preheat the broiler [grill] and broil the cheese toasts for 4-5 minutes, watching them carefully.
7. Toss the chicory with the dressing. Serve with the hot cheese toasts.

Choux au fromage

Cheese Puffs

🔪 00:20 00:10 to 00:12 🍲

American	Ingredients	Metric/Imperial
1 cup	Water	250 ml / 8 fl oz
½ cup	Butter	125 g / 4 oz
1¼ cups	Flour	150 g / 5 oz
5	Eggs	5
¾ cup	Grated gruyère cheese	75 g / 3 oz
	Grated nutmeg	
	Salt and pepper	

1. Preheat the oven to 425°F / 220°C / Gas Mark 7.
2. Place the water and butter in a saucepan and bring to a boil. Add the flour all at once, and stir until the dough comes away from the sides of the pan. Remove from the heat. Add one egg and mix vigorously and thoroughly. Add another egg and mix. Continue adding the eggs, incorporating each thoroughly before adding the next. Beat in the gruyère, a pinch of nutmeg, and salt and pepper to taste.
3. Using a pastry bag fitted with a ½ in / 1 cm tube, pipe the pastry in balls on a greased baking sheet. Bake for 10-12 minutes.

Bouchées au roquefort

Roquefort Puffs

00:40   00:15 to 00:18

American	Ingredients	Metric/Imperial
1 cup	Water	250 ml / 8 fl oz
¾ cup	Butter	175 g / 6 oz
	Salt	
1 cup	Flour	125 g / 4 oz
4	Eggs	4
½ lb	Roquefort cheese	250 g / 8 oz
1 tbsp	Crème fraîche	1 tbsp

1. Preheat the oven to 400°F / 200°C / Gas Mark 6.

2. Place the water, 5 tbsp [65 g / 2½ oz] of the butter and a pinch of salt in a saucepan. Bring to a boil. Add the flour all at once and stir until the dough comes away from the sides of the pan. Remove from the heat. Add one egg and mix thoroughly, then add another egg and mix. Continue adding the eggs, incorporating each thoroughly before adding the next.

3. Using a pastry bag fitted with a small tube, pipe the pastry onto a greased baking sheet. You should obtain 36 small heaps. Put into the oven and bake for 15-18 minutes or until risen and golden brown.

4. Turn off the oven and open the door. Leave the choux puffs inside for 2-3 minutes, then remove them.

5. Mix together the roquefort, remaining butter and crème fraîche, using a wooden spoon to obtain a very smooth mixture.

6. Split open the choux puffs with a knife and fill with the cheese mixture. Serve warm or cold.

Goat's cheese and walnut (Baked Goat's Cheese)

Barquettes chaudes au saumon

Hot Salmon Pastry Boats

	00:10		00:10	
	plus making pastry boats			
American	**Ingredients**		**Metric/Imperial**	
1½ tbsp	Butter		20 g / ¾ oz	
1½ tbsp	Flour		20 g / ¾ oz	
⅔ cup	Milk		150 ml / ¼ pint	
	Salt and pepper			
	Grated nutmeg			
1 (7 oz)	Can of pink salmon		1 (200 g / 7 oz)	
¾ cup	Grated gruyère cheese		75 g / 3 oz	
6	Baked pastry boats		6	

1. Preheat the oven to 400°F / 200°C / Gas Mark 6.
2. Melt the butter in a saucepan, add the flour and mix thoroughly. Cook for 1 minute. Gradually stir in the milk and cook, stirring continuously with a wooden spoon, until smooth and thickened. Season with salt, pepper and a pinch of nutmeg.
3. Drain and flake the salmon. Add to the sauce together with half the gruyère. Fill the pastry boats with the preparation and sprinkle with the remainder of the gruyère.
4. Place in the oven and bake until the gruyère on top is lightly browned. Serve immediately.

Feuilletés au roquefort

Roquefort Pastries

	00:25		00:15	
	plus thawing or making pastry			
American	**Ingredients**		**Metric/Imperial**	
¾ lb	Puff pastry		350 g / 12 oz	
½ lb	Roquefort cheese		250 g / 8 oz	
1	Egg		1	

1. If using frozen pastry, allow it to thaw. Preheat the oven to 450°F / 230°C / Gas Mark 8.
2. Roll out the pastry to a thickness of ⅛ in / 3 mm on a lightly floured surface. Cut into 16 rectangles measuring 3×4½ in / 7×11 cm.
3. Cut the roquefort cheese into 8 sticks the thickness of a finger. Place on 8 of the pastry rectangles.
4. Beat the egg. Brush the egg around the edges of the pastry rectangles on which the cheese has been placed.
5. Mark the remaining 8 pastry rectangles with a lattice pattern using the point of a knife. Lay these rectangles over the cheese and press with your fingers so that the pastry edges stick together. Brush the tops with beaten egg.
6. Place the rectangle on a lightly buttered baking sheet and bake for 10 minutes. Open the oven door and, leaving it ajar, continue baking for another 5 minutes.
7. Serve hot or warm.

Bouchées à la reine 🍳🍳🍳

Chicken Vol-au-Vents

🔪 00:30   01:00 🍲

American	Ingredients	Metric/Imperial
1 quart	Water	1 l / 1¾ pints
1	Onion	1
1	Carrot	1
1	Bouquet garni	1
	Salt and pepper	
2	Chicken wings	2
5 oz	Button mushrooms	150 g / 5 oz
	Lemon juice	
1	Small piece of veal sweetbread	1
½ cup	Butter	125 g / 4 oz
¼ cup	Flour	4 tbsp
	Grated nutmeg	
6	Baked patty shells (vol-au-vent cases)	6
3	Egg yolks	3
½ cup	Crème fraîche	125 ml / 4 fl oz
6	Small chicken dumplings	6

1. Put the water into a saucepan. Add the onion and carrot, both peeled, the bouquet garni and salt and pepper to taste. Bring to a boil and simmer until the carrot is tender.

2. Discard the bouquet garni. Add the chicken wings and leave to cook for 20 minutes.

3. Drain the chicken wings, reserving the cooking liquid. Discard the skin and bones and dice the meat. Strain the cooking liquid.

4. Preheat the oven to 400°F / 200°C / Gas Mark 6.

5. Slice the mushrooms and sprinkle with lemon juice to prevent them from discoloring.

6. Drop the veal sweetbread into a pan of boiling salted water and blanch for 10 minutes. Drain. Remove all gristle and dice.

7. Melt the butter in a thick-bottomed saucepan and stir in the flour. Gradually add three-quarters of the reserved chicken cooking liquid. Bring to a boil, stirring until thickened. Add the chicken, sweetbread, mushrooms and a pinch of nutmeg. Simmer over a gentle heat until well reduced and thickened.

8. Meanwhile, arrange the pastry cases on a baking sheet and heat through in the oven for 5 minutes.

9. Mix together the egg yolks and crème fraîche. Remove the saucepan from the heat and add the cream mixture. Stir thoroughly. Add the quenelles, sliced. Return to a low heat and cook gently, stirring, until hot. Do not allow to boil.

10. Fill the hot pastry cases with the chicken filling and serve.

Vol-au-vent

Sweetbread Vol-au-Vent

00:30　　　　　　　　00:50

American	Ingredients	Metric/Imperial
1½ lb	Veal sweetbreads	750 g / 1½ lb
	Salt and pepper	
1	Calf's brain	1
1 tbsp	Vinegar	1 tbsp
14 oz	Button mushrooms	400 g / 14 oz
10 tbsp	Butter	150 g / 5 oz
1	Carrot	1
2	Shallots	2
3 tbsp	Flour	3 tbsp
1 tbsp	Tomato paste [purée]	1 tbsp
2 cups	Chicken stock	500 ml / ¾ pint
1¼ cups	Madeira wine	300 ml / ½ pint
2 tbsp	Oil	2 tbsp
5 tbsp	Brandy	5 tbsp
1	Large patty shell (vol-au-vent case)	1
1	Slice of cooked ham	1
1	Egg yolk	1
½ cup	Crème fraîche	125 ml / 4 fl oz

1. Put the sweetbreads in a saucepan of cold, salted water, bring to a boil, and simmer for 5 minutes. Drain and cool in cold water, then trim off any tough portions and outer membranes. Cut into large dice.

2. Wash the brain, and soak for 15 minutes in cold water to which the vinegar has been added. Drain and remove all fiberlike membranes and threads. Rinse and cut into dice.

3. Thinly slice the mushrooms. Melt 2 tablespoons [25 g / 1 oz] of the butter in a saucepan, add the mushrooms and cook until all the moisture has evaporated. Set aside.

4. Peel and dice the carrot. Peel and thinly slice the shallots. Melt 2 tablespoons [25 g / 1 oz] butter in another saucepan and add the carrot and shallots. Fry gently until softened, then sprinkle on 2 tablespoons of the flour and cook for a few moments, stirring.

5. Add the tomato paste, chicken stock and madeira. Season to taste with salt and pepper. Bring to a boil, then reduce the heat and leave to simmer gently for 20 minutes.

6. Leave the sauce to cool, then remove any fat which has risen to the surface. Strain the sauce.

7. Preheat the oven to 300°F / 150°C / Gas Mark 2.

8. Coat the diced sweetbreads with the remaining flour. Heat the oil and 2 tablespoons [25 g / 1 oz] butter in a frying pan, add the sweetbreads and brown on all sides for 10 minutes. Season with salt and pepper. Add the brandy and set it alight, then add the mushrooms and madeira sauce. Cover and leave to cook for 15 minutes over a gentle heat.

9. Meanwhile, heat the pastry case in the oven.

10. Melt the remaining butter in a frying pan, add the diced brain and cook until browned, for 5 minutes. Dice the ham. Add the brain and ham to the sweetbread mixture.

11. Mix the egg yolk in a bowl with the crème fraîche. Add to the sweetbread mixture, off the heat, then use to fill the hot pastry case. Serve immediately.

Friands à la viande

Meat Pastries

	00:20		00:45	
	plus making or thawing pastry			

American	Ingredients	Metric/Imperial
14 oz	Puff pastry	400 g / 14 oz
3	Shallots	3
5 oz	Button mushrooms	150 g / 5 oz
½ lb	Boneless breast of veal	250 g / 8 oz
½ lb	Smoked bacon	250 g / 8 oz
1	Bunch of fresh parsley	1
5 tbsp	Crème fraîche	5 tbsp
2 tbsp	Brandy	2 tbsp
	Salt and pepper	
2 tbsp	Butter	25 g / 1 oz
1	Egg	1

1. If using frozen pastry, allow it to thaw. Peel and chop the shallots. Chop the mushrooms. Grind [mince] the breast of veal, bacon and parsley. Mix the veal, bacon, parsley and mushrooms together. Add the crème fraîche, brandy and salt and pepper to taste.
2. Heat the butter in a frying pan, add the shallots and cook gently over a low heat, stirring frequently until softened. Add to the veal mixture.
3. Preheat the oven to 425°F / 220°C / Gas Mark 7.
4. Roll out the pastry to ⅛ in / 3 mm thick and cut into 6 squares. Divide the filling between the pastry squares and roll up to enclose the filling completely. Lightly moisten the edges to seal. Using a pointed knife, score the top of the pastries.
5. Break the egg into a bowl, beat it and brush the pastries with beaten egg. Arrange them on a baking sheet, and bake for 25-30 minutes. Serve very hot.

Tarte à la moutarde

Mustard Cheese Tart

	00:25	00:40 to 00:50	
	plus thawing or making pastry		

American	Ingredients	Metric/Imperial
¾ lb	Puff pastry	350 g / 12 oz
6	Tomatoes	6
5 tbsp	Dijon mustard	5 tbsp
5 oz	Gruyère cheese	150 g / 5 oz

1. Preheat the oven to 450°F / 230°C / Gas Mark 8. Thaw the pastry if using frozen.
2. Peel the tomatoes (first plunging them into boiling water for 10 seconds), then cut into quarters and remove the seeds.
3. Roll out the pastry to a thickness of ⅛ in / 3 mm and use to line a buttered, lightly floured 10 in / 25 cm quiche or flan dish or pan. Spread the bottom with the mustard. Thinly slice the gruyère cheese and arrange over the mustard. Cover with the tomato quarters.
4. Bake for 40-50 minutes.

Tarte aux épinards

Spinach Tart

	00:20	00:50
	plus thawing or making pastry	

American	Ingredients	Metric/Imperial
¾ lb	Puff pastry	350 g / 12 oz
1 lb	Spinach	500 g / 1 lb
	Salt and pepper	
	Grated nutmeg	
5 tbsp	Butter	65 g / 2½ oz
1 tbsp	Flour	2 tbsp
1 cup	Crème fraîche	250 ml / 8 fl oz
4	Eggs	4

1. Preheat the oven to 425°F / 220°C / Gas Mark 7. Thaw the pastry if using frozen.

2. Trim the stalks off the spinach. Wash, then cook in boiling salted water until tender. Drain and, when cool enough to handle, squeeze out excess moisture. Chop the spinach finely or process in a food processor until coarse-fine (not a purée). Season with a pinch of grated nutmeg, and salt and pepper to taste.

3. Melt the butter in a heavy saucepan and add the flour. Cook, stirring, for 1 minute, then add the crème fraîche. Allow to thicken, stirring constantly. Season to taste with salt and pepper. Remove from the heat and add the beaten eggs. Mix two-thirds of this sauce with the spinach, and taste and adjust the seasoning.

4. Roll out the pastry thinly and use to line a buttered and floured 10 in / 25 cm quiche or flan dish or pan. Prick the bottom with a fork. Pour in the spinach mixture, and cover with the rest of the egg sauce.

5. Bake for 15 minutes or until the filling is firm and set. Turn off the oven and leave the tart in the oven for about 5-10 minutes longer. Serve warm or cold.

Tarte aux bettes

Swiss Chard Tart

	00:45	00:45
	plus thawing or making pastry	

American	Ingredients	Metric/Imperial
¾ lb	Puff pastry	350 g / 12 oz
2 lb	Swiss chard or beet tops [spinach beet]	1 kg / 2 lb
6 tbsp	Butter	75 g / 3 oz
	Grated nutmeg	
	Salt and pepper	
¾ lb	Onions	350 g / 12 oz
¾ lb	Tomatoes	350 g / 12 oz
2	Garlic cloves	2
1 tsp	Dried thyme	1 tsp
¾ cup	Grated gruyère cheese	75 g / 3 oz

1. Thaw the pastry if using frozen. Preheat the oven to 450°F / 230°C / Gas Mark 8.

2. Roll out the pastry and use to line a buttered and floured 10 in / 25 cm quiche or flan dish or pan. Prick the bottom with a fork and keep cool.

3. Remove the ribs from the chard, wash and cut them into thin strips. Melt 2 tablespoons [25 g / 1 oz] of the butter in a saucepan, add the chard and cook until all the moisture has evaporated. Add a pinch of grated nutmeg, and salt and pepper to taste.

4. Peel and slice the onions. Melt 2 tablespoons [25 g / 1 oz] of the butter in a frying pan, add the onions and cook until softened, without letting them turn brown.

5. Peel the tomatoes (first plunging them into boiling water for 10 seconds), then remove the seeds. Cut the flesh into pieces. Melt the remaining butter in a saucepan, add the tomatoes and cook until reduced to a pulp.

6. Peel and crush the garlic. Add to the tomatoes with the onions and thyme. Season to taste with salt and pepper.

7. Cover the bottom of the pastry case with half the tomato mixture. Sprinkle with half of the grated gruyère cheese and arrange the chard in an even layer on top. Cover with the remaining tomato mixture, and sprinkle with the rest of the cheese.

8. Bake for 20 minutes, then lower the heat to 350°F / 180°C / Gas Mark 4 and bake for 25 minutes. Serve warm or cold.

Pissaladière

Pizza Tart

	00:30		01:15	
	plus thawing or making pastry			

American	Ingredients	Metric/Imperial
½ lb	Puff pastry	250 g / 8 oz
½ lb	Onions	250 g / 8 oz
1 tbsp	Olive oil	1 tbsp
	Salt and pepper	
2 lb	Tomatoes	1 kg / 2 lb
2 tbsp	Tomato paste [purée]	2 tbsp
1 (2 oz)	Can of anchovies in oil	1 (50 g / 2 oz)
	Dried marjoram	
15	Black olives, pitted [stoned]	15

1. Preheat the oven to 400°F / 200°C / Gas Mark 6. If using frozen pastry, allow it to thaw.
2. Peel the onions and cut into thin slices. Heat the oil in a saucepan, add the onions and fry gently until beginning to brown. Season lightly with pepper and a very little salt. Put to one side.
3. Slice the tomatoes.
4. Roll out the pastry to a thickness of ⅛ in / 3 mm, and use to line a buttered 10 in / 25 cm quiche or flan pan or dish.
5. Spread the tomato paste over the bottom of the pastry case, then put the onions, tomato slices and anchovy fillets on top (save the oil from the anchovies). Sprinkle with a little marjoram, pepper and the oil from the anchovies.
6. Bake for 20 minutes. Garnish with the olives.

Tarte au Maroilles

Maroilles Cheese Tart

	00:30		00:35	
	plus making pastry and standing time			

American	Ingredients	Metric/Imperial
1 quantity	Basic short pastry	1 quantity
½	Maroilles or similar cheese (not too fresh)	½
½ lb	Soft cream cheese	250 g / 8 oz
1 cup	Thick crème fraîche	250 ml / 8 fl oz
4	Eggs	4
	Pepper	

1. Roll out the pastry and use to line a buttered 10 in / 25 cm quiche or flan dish or pan. Set aside.
2. Remove the crust from the maroilles cheese. Crumble the cheese into a bowl, and add the cream cheese and crème fraîche. Mix to obtain a smooth consistency. Add the eggs one by one, and season to taste with pepper. Leave to rest for about 30 minutes in a cool place.
3. Preheat the oven to 425°F / 220°C / Gas Mark 7.
4. Fill the pastry case with the cheese mixture. Bake for about 35 minutes. Watch over the tart, and make sure that the top does not burn. If it is browning too much, cover it with foil. Serve hot.

Tarte aux oignons

Onion Tart

| | 00:45 plus chilling | 00:50 |

American	Ingredients	Metric/Imperial
½ cup + 2 tbsp	Butter	150 g / 5 oz
	Salt and pepper	
2 cups + 2 tbsp	Flour	250 g / 8 oz + 2 tbsp
4	Egg yolks	4
1 lb	Onions	500 g / 1 lb
2 cups	Milk	500 ml / ¾ pint
	Grated nutmeg	

1. Cut ½ cup [125 g / 4 oz] of the butter into small pieces, and leave to soften at room temperature. Mix a pinch of salt, 2 cups [250 g / 8 oz] of the flour and 1 egg yolk in a bowl. Add the softened butter and mix to a dough. Roll the dough into a ball, and chill for 1 hour.
2. Preheat the oven to 425°F / 220°C / Gas Mark 7.
3. Roll out the dough thinly and use to line a buttered 10 in / 25 cm quiche or flan dish or pan. Prick the bottom with a fork.
4. Peel and slice the onions. Melt the remaining butter in a saucepan, add the onions and fry over a low heat, so that they will be softened before they start to brown.
5. Sprinkle the onions with the remaining flour and stir well to mix. Add three-quarters of the milk, and bring to a boil, stirring continuously. Add the rest of the milk. Remove from the heat and beat in the remaining egg yolks, one at a time. Season with salt and pepper to taste and a pinch of nutmeg.
6. Pour the onion mixture into the pastry case. Bake for 35-40 minutes. Serve warm.

Tourte au jambon

Ham Pie

| | 00:30 plus thawing or making pastry | 01:00 to 01:15 |

American	Ingredients	Metric/Imperial
1¼ lb	Puff pastry	625 g / 1¼ lb
6	Thin slices of cooked ham	6
14 oz	Emmental cheese	400 g / 14 oz
1	Egg	1

1. Preheat the oven to 450°F / 230°C / Gas Mark 8.
2. Roll out half the pastry to a thickness of about ⅛ in / 3 mm. Cut out a 10 in / 25 cm round and place it on a lightly oiled and floured baking sheet.
3. Arrange 3 slices of ham (with the fat cut off) on the pastry base. Cover with half of the emmental cheese, cut into thin slices, then place another 3 slices of ham on top of the cheese. Finally add a layer of the remaining cheese cut into thin slices. Leave a clear border of ½ in / 1 cm around the edge of the pastry round.
4. Roll out the other half of the pastry and cut out a round as before. Moisten the edge with beaten egg and place this round

on top of the first one. Press down the edge to seal the pastry rounds together, and crimp or flute the edge.

5. Glaze the top with beaten egg. Prick in 3 or 4 places with a fork, and draw a pattern with the tip of a knife.

6. Bake for 30 minutes, then reduce the heat to 425°F / 220°C / Gas Mark 7, and bake for a further 30-45 minutes. Serve warm.

Tourte aux morilles

Morel Pie

	00:20	00:40
	plus thawing or making pastry	

American	Ingredients	Metric/Imperial
2 oz	Dried morels or other mushrooms	50 g / 2 oz
1¼ lb	Puff pastry	625 g / 1¼ lb
1	Egg	1
1	Onion	1
¼ cup	Butter	50 g / 2 oz
1 cup	Crème fraîche	250 ml / 8 fl oz
	Salt and pepper	

1. Put the dried morels into warm water to soak for 2 hours.

2. Thaw the pastry if using frozen. Preheat the oven to 425°F / 220°C / Gas Mark 7.

3. Roll out half the pastry to about ⅛ in / 3 mm. Use to line a buttered 10 in / 25 cm quiche or flan dish or pan. Line the pastry with a sheet of wax [greaseproof] paper and fill the dish with dried beans. Roll out the rest of the pastry and lay over the beans, making a pastry lid. Moisten the edge, twist it up and make oblique cuts in it. Draw lozenges on the top with a pointed knife, and glaze with beaten egg.

4. Bake for 40 minutes.

5. Meanwhile, peel and chop the onion. Heat the butter in a saucepan, add the onion and cook gently until softened. Do not allow it to turn brown.

6. Drain the morels and cut into pieces if large. Add to the onion and cook until the moisture has completely evaporated.

7. Add the crème fraîche, and simmer until it thickens. Season to taste with salt and pepper.

8. To serve, carefully remove the hot pastry lid with a knife and take out the paper and beans. Pour in the morel mixture and replace the pastry lid. Serve hot.

Morels

Flamiche aux poireaux

Leek Pie

⟐━━	01:15		00:30 ⟐
	plus making pastry		

American	Ingredients	Metric/Imperial
12	Leeks	12
¼ cup	Butter	50 g / 2 oz
	Salt and pepper	
1 quantity	Basic short pastry	1 quantity
2	Egg yolks	2
3 tbsp	Crème fraîche	3 tbsp

1. Trim the roots off the leeks, remove the damaged ends of the green leaves, and split the leeks into quarters. Clean under cold water, separating the layers. Cut into thin slices crosswise. Place in a saucepan with the butter and salt and pepper to taste and cook over a gentle heat for 1 hour, stirring occasionally.
2. Preheat the oven to 450°F / 230°C / Gas Mark 8.
3. Divide the pastry into 2 unequal portions. Roll out the larger portion, and use to line a deep pie pan.
4. Beat one of the egg yolks with the crème fraîche. Add to the cooked leeks and stir well. Pour into the pastry case.
5. Roll out the remaining pastry and lay it over the leeks. Moisten the pastry edges with a little egg white and press them together to seal. Brush the top with the beaten egg yolk.
6. Bake for 30 minutes. Serve warm.

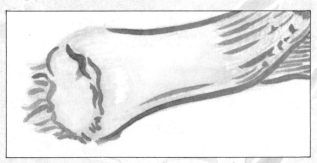

Quiche Lorraine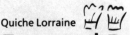

Egg and Bacon Quiche

⟐━━	00:20		00:20 ⟐
	plus making pastry		

American	Ingredients	Metric/Imperial
1 quantity	Basic short pastry	1 quantity
¼ lb	Smoked bacon	125 g / 4 oz
3	Eggs	3
½ cup	Crème fraîche	125 ml / 4 fl oz
1¼ cups	Grated gruyère cheese	150 g / 5 oz
	Salt and pepper	
	Grated nutmeg	

1. Preheat the oven to 450°F / 230°C / Gas Mark 8.
2. Roll out the pastry and use to line a buttered 10 in / 25 cm quiche or flan pan or dish. Prick the bottom with a fork.
3. Cut the bacon into dice and sprinkle over the bottom of the pastry case.

4. Break the eggs into a bowl and beat with the crème fraîche, grated gruyère cheese, a pinch of salt, a pinch of grated nutmeg, and pepper to taste. Pour this mixture over the bacon in the pastry case.

5. Bake for 20 minutes and serve very hot.

Crêpes farcies

Stuffed Crêpes

	00:25	00:20 to 00:25	
	plus standing time		

American	Ingredients	Metric/Imperial
2	Eggs	2
1¼ cups	Flour	150 g / 5 oz
1¼ cups	Milk	250 ml / 8 fl oz
1 cup	Beer	150 ml / ¼ pint
	Salt and pepper	
10 tbsp	Butter	150 g / 5 oz
¼ lb	Cooked ham or	125 g / 4 oz
3	Eggs	3
1 lb	Spinach or beet tops	150 g / 5 oz
	Grated nutmeg	
1¼ cups	Grated gruyère cheese	150 g / 5 oz
½ cup	Crème fraîche	125 ml / 4 fl oz

1. Prepare the crêpe batter: break the 2 eggs into a mixing bowl, beat them together and add the flour. Stir with a wooden spoon to obtain a smooth batter and thin it out gradually with the milk. Blend thoroughly. Add the beer and a pinch of salt. Gently melt 3 tablespoons [40 g / 1½ oz] of the butter in a saucepan. Incorporate it into the batter and leave to stand for 2 hours.

2. Melt a small piece of butter in a crêpe or frying pan. Add a ladleful of batter and tilt the frying pan in all directions to spread the batter evenly over the bottom. Cook over medium heat for 1½-2 minutes, then turn the crêpe over and cook the other side. Continue making crêpes in this way until all the batter has been used up.

3. If preparing the crêpes the day before, wrap them in foil, interleaving each one with wax [greaseproof] paper and store in the refrigerator.

4. Preheat the oven to 400°F / 200°C / Gas Mark 6.

5. Chop the ham, or hard-cook the eggs in boiling water for 10 minutes. Drain, run under cold water and remove the shells. Chop the eggs.

6. Remove any damaged leaves and large ribs from the spinach or beet tops, rinse and toss into a saucepan of boiling salted water. Leave to cook for 5 minutes after boiling has resumed, then drain. Squeeze out excess moisture, then chop coarsely.

7. Melt 2 tablespoons [25 g / 1 oz] butter in a saucepan, add the spinach and leave to cook until all the vegetable water has evaporated. Add a pinch of nutmeg, ½ cup [50 g / 2 oz] of the gruyère, the chopped eggs or ham, and salt and pepper to taste. Mix thoroughly.

8. Fill the crêpes with the spinach mixture and roll them up. Arrange very tightly in a buttered ovenproof dish. Coat them with the crème fraîche, scatter over the remaining cheese and a few small pieces of butter. Bake for about 25 minutes.

Ficelles picardes

Ham and Mushroom Crêpes

	00:20		00:30
	plus making crêpes		

American	Ingredients	Metric/Imperial
1 lb	Button mushrooms	500 g / 1 lb
2 tbsp	Butter	25 g / 1 oz
1 cup	Crème fraîche	250 ml / 8 fl oz
1 cup	Grated gruyère cheese	125 g / 4 oz
	Salt and pepper	
6	Sliced of cooked ham	6
6	Crêpes	6

1. Preheat the oven to 400°F / 200°C / Gas Mark 6.
2. Chop the mushrooms. Heat the butter in a frying pan, add the mushrooms and cook until all their moisture has evaporated. Remove from the heat and add 1 tablespoon of the crème fraîche and 1-2 tablespoons of the gruyère. Add salt and pepper to taste.
3. Place a slice of ham on each crêpe. Cover with the mushroom mixture and roll up. Place the crêpes very close together in a buttered ovenproof dish. Pour over the remaining crème fraîche, which has been lightly seasoned with salt and pepper, and sprinkle with the remaining gruyère cheese. Place in the oven and bake for 30 minutes.

Crêpes aux champignons

Mushroom Crêpes

	00:30		00:45
	plus standing time		

American	Ingredients	Metric/Imperial
2	Eggs	2
1¼ cups + 3 tbsp	Flour	190 g / 6½ oz
3¼ cups	Milk	750 ml / 1¼ pints
1 cup	Beer	150 ml / ¼ pint
	Salt and pepper	
¾ cup	Butter	175 g / 6 oz
	Grated nutmeg	
14 oz	Button mushrooms	400 g / 14 oz
2	Shallots	2
1	Garlic clove	1
1 cup	Grated gruyère cheese	125 g / 4 oz

1. Prepare the crêpe batter: break the eggs into a mixing bowl, beat them together and add 1¼ cups [150 g / 5 oz] of the flour. Stir with a wooden spoon to obtain a smooth batter and thin it out gradually with 1¼ cups [250 ml / 8 fl oz] of the milk. Blend thoroughly. Add the beer and a pinch of salt. Gently melt 3 tablespoons [40 g / 1½ oz] of the butter in a saucepan. Incorporate it into the batter and leave to stand for 2 hours.
2. Meanwhile, melt 3 tablespoons [40 g / 1½ oz] of the butter in a saucepan, stir in the remaining flour and cook for

1 minute. Gradually stir in the remaining milk and then, continuing to stir, leave to thicken over a gentle heat for about 8-10 minutes. Season with salt, pepper and nutmeg to taste.

3. Finely chop the mushrooms. Peel and chop the shallots and garlic. Heat 3 tablespoons [40 g / 1½ oz] butter in a small frying pan, add the mushrooms, shallots and garlic and leave to cook over a gentle heat, stirring frequently, until all the liquid has evaporated. Add salt and pepper to taste.

4. Add half the sauce and mix thoroughly. Set aside.

5. Preheat the oven to 475°F / 240°C / Gas Mark 9.

6. Melt a small piece of butter in a crêpe or frying pan. Add a ladleful of batter and tilt the frying pan in all directions to spread the batter evenly over the bottom. Cook over a medium heat for 1½-2 minutes, then turn the crêpe over and cook the other side. Continue making crêpes in this way until all the batter has been used up.

7. Fill the crêpes with the mushroom mixture and roll them up. Arrange very tightly in a buttered baking dish. Cover them with the remainder of the sauce and dot with small pieces of butter. Sprinkle with gruyère.

8. Bake for 5-10 minutes and serve hot.

Galettes de blé noir

Buckwheat Crêpes

	00:15 plus standing time		00:05 per crêpe	
American	**Ingredients**		**Metric/Imperial**	
2¾ cups	Buckwheat flour		300 g / 11 oz	
	Salt			
7	Eggs		7	
3 cups	Water		750 ml / 1¼ pints	
½ cup	Butter		125 g / 4 oz	
6	Slices of cooked ham		6	
1¼ cups	Grated gruyère cheese		150 g / 5 oz	

1. Combine the flour and a pinch of salt in a mixing bowl. Add one of the eggs, then pour in the water in a trickle, beating to obtain a smooth batter. Leave to rest for 30 minutes.

2. Grease a crêpe or frying pan or griddle with a little butter. Pour on a spoonful of batter, spreading it out well. Cook the crêpe for 2 minutes, then turn it over with a spatula. Put a pat of butter on it, then break an egg on top and leave to cook for a few minutes. Season to taste with salt and pepper.

3. When the egg is cooked, put a slice of ham on the crêpe and sprinkle with grated gruyère cheese. Fold the crêpe into quarters and remove from the pan. Keep hot while you make 5 more crêpes in the same way.

Crêpes au roquefort

Roquefort Crêpes

00:15
plus standing time

00:30

American	Ingredients	Metric/Imperial
2	Eggs	2
1¼ cups	Flour	150 g / 5 oz
1¼ cups	Milk	250 ml / 8 fl oz
1 cup	Beer	150 ml / ¼ pint
	Salt and pepper	
½ cup	Butter	125 g / 4 oz
2 oz	Roquefort cheese	50 g / 2 oz
	Melted butter for serving	

1. Prepare the crêpe batter: break the eggs into a mixing bowl, beat them together and add the flour. Stir with a wooden spoon to obtain a smooth batter and thin it out gradually with the milk. Blend thoroughly. Add the beer and a pinch of salt. Gently melt 3 tbsp [40 g / 1½ oz] of the butter in a saucepan. Incorporate it into the batter and leave to stand for 2 hours.

2. Finely crush the roquefort using a fork to obtain a smooth cream. Heat ¼ cup [50 g / 2 oz] of the butter and incorporate it into the roquefort cream. Add this mixture to the crêpe batter and whisk until very smooth. If the batter is too thick, add a little more beer.

3. Melt a small piece of butter in a crêpe or frying pan. Add a ladleful of the batter and tilt the pan in all directions to spread the batter evenly over the bottom. Cook over a medium heat for 1½-2 minutes, then turn the crêpe over and cook the other side. Continue making crêpes until the batter has been used up.

4. As each crêpe is cooked, coat it with a little melted butter before rolling it up. Keep warm between 2 plates placed over a saucepan of boiling water.

Crêpes à la florentine

Spinach Crêpes

00:20
plus standing time

00:30

American	Ingredients	Metric/Imperial
2	Eggs	2
1¼ cups	Flour	150 g / 5 oz
1¼ cups	Milk	250 ml / 8 fl oz
1 cup	Beer	150 ml / ¼ pint
	Salt and pepper	
6 tbsp	Butter	75 g / 3 oz
2 lb	Fresh spinach	1 kg / 2 lb
1¼ cups	Thick crème fraîche	300 ml / ½ pint
1 cup	Grated gruyère cheese	125 g / 4 oz

1. Prepare the crêpe batter: break the eggs into a mixing bowl, beat them together and add the flour. Stir with a wooden spoon to obtain a smooth batter and thin it out gradually with the milk. Blend thoroughly. Add the beer and a pinch of salt. Gently melt half of the butter in a saucepan. Incorporate it into the batter and leave to stand for 2 hours.

2. Preheat the oven to 450°F / 230°C / Gas Mark 8.

3. Carefully clean the spinach and remove the stalks. Add to a saucepan of boiling salted water and cook for 10 minutes. Drain, run under cold water and squeeze in your hands to extract all the water. Coarsely chop the spinach.

4. Put half the crème fraîche and half the gruyère into a small frying pan. Add the spinach and pepper to taste, and blend thoroughly. Leave to warm, with the lid on, over a gentle heat.

5. Melt a small piece of butter in a crêpe or frying pan. Add a ladleful of the batter and tilt the pan in all directions to spread the batter evenly over the bottom. Cook over a medium heat for 1½-2 minutes, then turn the crêpe over and cook the other side. Continue making crêpes in this way until all the batter has been used up.

6. Fill the crêpes with the spinach mixture and roll them up. Arrange in a buttered baking dish. Heat the remainder of the crème fraîche in a small saucepan and use to coat the crêpes. Sprinkle with the remainder of the grated cheese.

7. Place in the oven and bake until the top is golden brown and the crêpes are piping hot.

Soufflé au jambon

Ham Soufflé

00:30 to 00:35   00:30

American	Ingredients	Metric/Imperial
¼ lb	Cooked ham	125 g / 4 oz
¼ lb	Button mushrooms	125 g / 4 oz
5 tbsp	Butter	65 g / 2½ oz
2½ cups	Milk	600 ml / 1 pint
	Grated nutmeg	
	Salt and pepper	
¼ cup	Flour	50 g / 2 oz
5	Eggs, separated	5

1. Preheat the oven to 400°F / 200°C / Gas Mark 6.

2. Cut the fat off the cooked ham, and chop the ham very finely. Chop the mushrooms. Melt 1 tablespoon of the butter in a frying pan, add the mushrooms and cook, stirring occasionally, until all the moisture has evaporated. Mix the mushrooms with the chopped ham.

3. Season the milk with a pinch of nutmeg and salt and pepper to taste. Bring to a boil.

4. Melt the remaining butter in a heavy saucepan and add the flour. Stir well, then gradually add the boiling milk, stirring constantly. Cook for about 10 minutes, stirring.

5. Remove from the heat, and add the egg yolks, one by one, blending each in thoroughly before adding the next. Add the ham and mushrooms and mix well together.

6. Beat the egg whites until stiff and gently fold them into the ham mixture. Spoon into a well-buttered 8 in / 20 cm diameter soufflé dish. The dish should be two-thirds full.

7. Bake for 10 minutes, then raise the temperature to 425°F / 220°C / Gas Mark 7, and bake for 20 minutes longer. Serve immediately.

Soufflé au bleu

Blue Cheese Soufflé

American	Ingredients	Metric/Imperial
2 cups	Milk	500 ml / ¾ pint
	Salt and pepper	
¼ cup	Butter	50 g / 2 oz
¼ cup	Flour	50 g / 2 oz
½ lb	Auvergne or other blue cheese	250 g / 8 oz
6	Eggs, separated	6

1. Preheat the oven to 350°F / 180°C / Gas Mark 4.

2. Season the milk with salt and pepper to taste and bring to a boil. Melt the butter in a heavy saucepan and add the flour. Stir well, then gradually add the boiling milk, stirring constantly. Cook for about 10 minutes, stirring.

3. Remove from the heat, and add the crumbled blue cheese and the egg yolks, one at a time.

4. Beat the egg whites to stiff peaks, then fold them gently into the cheese mixture. Spoon into a buttered 8 in / 20 cm diameter soufflé dish. The dish should be two-thirds full.

5. Bake for 10 minutes, then raise the temperature to 425°F / 220°C / Gas Mark 7 and bake for 20 minutes longer. Serve immediately.

Cook's tip: do not open the oven door while the soufflé is cooking. If it comes into contact with cold air, it is liable to collapse.

Gruyère and nutmeg (Cheese Soufflé)

Soufflé au fromage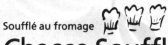

Cheese Soufflé

🔪 00:25	00:25 to 00:30 🍲	
American	**Ingredients**	**Metric/Imperial**
2½ cups	Milk	600 ml / 1 pint
	Salt and pepper	
¼ cup	Butter	50 g / 2 oz
¼ cup	Flour	50 g / 2 oz
	Grated nutmeg	
5	Eggs, separated	5
¾ cup	Grated gruyère cheese	75 g / 3 oz

1. Preheat the oven to 350°F / 180°C / Gas Mark 4.
2. Season the milk with salt and pepper to taste and bring to a boil. Melt the butter in a heavy saucepan and add the flour. Stir well, then gradually add the boiling milk, stirring constantly. Cook for about 10 minutes, stirring. Add a pinch of grated nutmeg.
3. Remove from the heat and add the egg yolks one by one, blending each in thoroughly before adding the next. Stir in the grated gruyère cheese.
4. Beat the egg whites until stiff and gently fold into the cheese mixture. Spoon into a buttered 8 in / 20 cm diameter soufflé dish. The dish should be two-thirds full.
5. Bake for 10 minutes, then raise the temperature to 425°F / 220°C / Gas Mark 7 and bake for 20 minutes longer. Serve immediately.

Fondue savoyarde

Savoy Fondue

🔪 00:20	00:20 to 00:25 🍲	
American	**Ingredients**	**Metric/Imperial**
1 lb	Emmental cheese	500 g / 1 lb
1 lb	Comté or similar cheese	500 g / 1 lb
1 lb	Beaufort or similar cheese	500 g / 1 lb
1	Garlic clove	1
1 quart	Dry white wine	1 l / 1¾ pints
	Pepper	
1 tbsp	Cornstarch [cornflour]	1 tbsp
⅔ cup	Kirsch	150 ml / ¼ pint
	French bread	

1. Remove any rind from the cheeses and cut them into thin slices.
2. Peel the garlic and rub the inside of a saucepan with it. Pour the wine into the saucepan, bring to a boil and add all the cheese. Stir until the cheese has completely melted. Add pepper to taste.
3. Dissolve the cornstarch in the kirsch. Pour into the saucepan and stir well until smooth and slightly thickened.
4. Cut the bread into cubes.
5. Put the saucepan on a spirit burner and serve immediately, with the bread cubes for dipping.

Beignets d'avocats

Avocado Fritters

	00:15 plus standing time		00:20

American	Ingredients	Metric/Imperial
2	Eggs	2
1 tsp	Salt	1 tsp
1¼ cups + 3 tbsp	Flour	150 g / 5 oz + 3 tbsp
	Pepper	
1 - 1½ cups	Beer	150 ml / ¼ pint
4	Avocados	4
	Oil for deep frying	
1	Egg white	1
	Lemon wedges	

1. Prepare the batter: whisk the whole eggs and salt in a mixing bowl and add 1¼ cups [150 g / 5 oz] of the flour and pepper to taste. Mix thoroughly. Gradually stir in the beer. Leave to stand for 2 hours.
2. Peel the avocados. Cut in half lengthwise, remove the seed and cut the flesh into ¾ in / 2 cm cubes. Coat in the remaining flour.
3. Heat oil for deep frying to 345°F / 175°C.
4. Beat the egg white into a firm snow and fold into the batter.
5. Dip the avocado cubes into the batter, then plunge into the oil. Cook until puffed and brown, then drain on paper towels. Serve hot, surrounded by lemon wedges.

Courgettes farcies

Stuffed Zucchini [Courgettes]

	00:20		00:30

American	Ingredients	Metric/Imperial
6	Zucchini [courgettes]	6
	Salt and pepper	
¾ lb	Cooked meat (pork, veal or beef)	350 g / 12 oz
4	Onions	4
2	Garlic cloves	2
1	Bunch of fresh parsley	1
2	Eggs	2
	Grated nutmeg	
½ cup	Grated gruyère cheese	50 g / 2 oz
¼ cup	Butter	50 g / 2 oz

1. Preheat the oven to 350°F / 180°C / Gas Mark 4.
2. Wipe the zucchini and cut them in half lengthwise. Remove most of the flesh with a small spoon and keep it in reserve.
3. Toss the zucchini shells into a saucepan of boiling salted water and cook for 2 minutes. Drain and run under cold water, then drain in a colander.

4. Grind [mince] together the cooked meat, peeled onions, peeled garlic cloves, parsley and the flesh from the zucchini. Add the eggs, a pinch of nutmeg, and salt and pepper to taste, mixing thoroughly with a fork.

5. Fill the zucchini shells with the stuffing and place them in a buttered baking dish. Sprinkle with the cheese and dot with small pieces of butter.

6. Place in the oven and bake for about 20 minutes. While they are cooking, baste the zucchini halves occasionally with the cooking juice.

Aubergines farcies

Stuffed Eggplants [Aubergines]

00:20   00:50

American	Ingredients	Metric/Imperial
3	Eggplants [aubergines]	3
⅔ cup	Olive oil	150 ml / ¼ pint
8	Large tomatoes	8
3	Onions	3
1	Shallot	1
3	Garlic cloves	3
1	Small bunch of fresh parsley	1
	Salt and pepper	
¾ cup	Fresh bread crumbs	40 g / 1 ½ oz
1 ¼ cups	Grated gruyère cheese	150 g / 5 oz

1. Preheat the oven to 475°F / 240°C / Gas Mark 9.

2. With a small pointed knife, remove the stalks from the eggplants. Split open the eggplants lengthwise. Cut all around the pulp, ⅛ in / 3 mm from the skin, without piercing the skin. Score deep elongated diamond shapes in the pulp. Put the eggplant halves on a baking sheet, sprinkle with a little of the olive oil and bake until the pulp pulls away from the skin completely.

3. Meanwhile, peel the tomatoes (first plunging them for 10 seconds into boiling water). Remove the seeds and chop the pulp coarsely. Peel and chop the onions, shallot and garlic.

4. Using a spoon, carefully remove the pulp from the eggplant halves. Set the shells of skin aside. Heat the rest of the oil in a small frying pan and add the eggplant pulp, onions, garlic, shallot, chopped parsley and tomatoes. Add salt and pepper to taste. Leave to cook, stirring from time to time, until all of the liquid from the vegetables has evaporated.

5. Add about 1 teaspoon of the bread crumbs to the vegetable mixture and adjust the seasoning if necessary. Stuff the eggplant skins with this preparation and sprinkle with the gruyère mixed with the remaining crumbs.

6. Place in the oven and bake for 5-10 minutes or until the tops are golden brown. Serve piping hot.

Small purple artichokes (Stuffed Artichokes, Provençal Style)

Royales à la tomate

Individual Tomato Custards

	00:40 plus chilling	00:45

American	Ingredients	Metric/Imperial
4	Large tomatoes	4
2	Garlic cloves	2
2	Shallots	2
2 tbsp	Olive oil	2 tbsp
1	Bouquet garni	1
1 tsp	Sugar	1 tsp
	Salt and pepper	
2 cups	Milk	500 ml / ¾ pint
3	Eggs	3
2	Egg yolks	2
1	Small bunch of fresh parsley	1
6	Black olives	6
6	Canned anchovy fillets	6

1. Peel the tomatoes (first plunging them into boiling water for 10 seconds). Remove the seeds and crush the flesh. Peel and crush the garlic. Peel and chop the shallots.
2. Heat the olive oil in a saucepan, add the shallots and cook gently until they begin to turn brown. Add the tomatoes, garlic, bouquet garni, sugar, and salt and pepper to taste. Stir well. Cover and leave to cook over a gentle heat for about 15 minutes.
3. Meanwhile, bring the milk to a boil. Beat the whole eggs and egg yolks together in a bowl, and add the boiling milk little by little. Chop the parsley and add to the custard.
4. If the tomato mixture is very liquid, boil it uncovered until excess moisture has evaporated. Discard the bouquet garni. Add the tomato mixture to the custard. Taste and adjust the seasoning.

5. Pour the mixture into 6 buttered ramekins and place them in a baking pan or wide shallow saucepan of simmering water. Cook for 45 minutes. Leave to cool for 2 hours.

6. To serve, unmold the tomato custards and garnish each with a black olive surrounded by an anchovy. Serve very cold.

Artichauts Barigoule

Stuffed Artichokes, Provençal Style

01:00   00:40

American	Ingredients	Metric/Imperial
6	Globe artichokes or	6
12	Small purple artichokes	12
	Lemon juice	
	Salt and pepper	
½ lb	Button mushrooms	250 g / 8 oz
¼ lb	Unsmoked bacon	125 g / 4 oz
3	Shallots	3
2 tbsp	Olive oil	2 tbsp
1 tbsp	Chopped fresh parsley	1 tbsp
2	Onions	2
2	Carrots	2
6	Thin slices of smoked bacon	6
⅔ cup	White wine	150 ml / ¼ pint
1	Bouquet garni	1

1. Trim the stalks from the artichokes and remove all the leaves. Dip the peeled hearts immediately in lemon juice to prevent them from turning black.

2. Put some salted water and a little lemon juice into a saucepan, add the artichoke hearts and bring to a boil. Leave to cook for 15-30 minutes or until tender but still firm. Drain and remove the hairy chokes.

3. Preheat the oven to 425°F / 220°C / Gas Mark 7.

4. Finely chop the mushrooms. Chop the unsmoked bacon. Peel and chop the shallots.

5. Heat 1 tablespoon of the oil in a frying pan, add the bacon, mushrooms, shallots, parsley, and salt and pepper to taste and cook, stirring, until lightly browned. Drain off excess fat.

6. Peel and chop the onions and carrots and brown them in the remaining olive oil in another pan.

7. Wrap each artichoke heart in a slice of smoked bacon. Top with the mushroom mixture and then with the carrot mixture. Arrange the hearts in a casserole.

8. Add the wine and bouquet garni and cover the casserole. Put the casserole into the oven and braise for 30-40 minutes. Remove the lid 10 minutes before cooking finishes for the sauce to reduce.

9. Remove the bouquet garni and serve.

Aubergines farcies aux champignons de Paris

Eggplants [Aubergines] with Mushrooms

00:10		00:25
American	**Ingredients**	**Metric/Imperial**
6	Eggplants [aubergines]	6
3 tbsp	Olive oil	3 tbsp
1½ lb	Button mushrooms	750 g / 1½ lb
4	Onions	4
2	Garlic cloves	2
1	Small bunch of fresh parsley	1
¾ lb	Sausage meat	350 g / 12 oz
2	Egg yolks	2
	Salt and pepper	

1. Preheat the oven to 425°F / 220°C / Gas Mark 7.
2. Using a small pointed knife, remove the stalks from the eggplants. Split open the eggplants lengthwise. Using a sharp knife, score deep elongated diamond shapes in the pulp. Place the halves in an ovenproof dish. Sprinkle with a little of the olive oil, place in the oven and bake for 10 minutes.
3. Meanwhile, prepare the stuffing. Cut the mushrooms into small cubes. Cook gently for about 5 minutes in a little olive oil.
4. Peel and finely chop the onions and garlic. Chop the parsley.
5. Combine the mushrooms, onions, garlic and parsley in a mixing bowl. Add the sausage meat and egg yolks and mix well. Season with salt and pepper to taste.
6. Take the eggplants out of the oven. Using a grapefruit knife, cut all around the pulp ½ in / 1 cm from the skin, and without piercing the skin. Distribute the stuffing over the entire length of each half.
7. Put the dish back into the oven and bake for a further 15 minutes. Serve hot.

Raclette

Melted Cheese Potatoes

00:08 to 00:10		00:30
American	**Ingredients**	**Metric/Imperial**
4 lb	Potatoes	2 kg / 4 lb
	Salt and pepper	
½ lb	Raclette or other melting cheese	250 g / 8 oz
	Pickled onions	
	Small dill pickles [gherkins]	

1. Place the unpeeled potatoes in a saucepan of cold salted water and bring to a boil. Simmer for 25 minutes.
2. Meanwhile, preheat the broiler.
3. Cut the cheese into slices as long as a plate, and ⅛ in / 3 mm thick. Put each slice on an ovenproof plate.
4. Drain the potatoes and keep hot.

5. Put 2-3 plates under the broiler and cook until the cheese melts and turns a light golden brown. Take the plates to the table immediately, and put some more under the broiler.
6. Serve the cheese very hot, with plenty of pepper, the potatoes, pickled onions and pickles.

Small dill pickles (gherkins) and pickled onions

Fonds d'artichaut farcis
Stuffed Artichoke Hearts

00:30   01:00

American	Ingredients	Metric/Imperial
6	Large globe artichokes	6
	Lemon juice	
	Salt and pepper	
½ lb	Cooked ham	250 g / 8 oz
½ lb	Button mushrooms	250 g / 8 oz
5 tbsp	Butter	65 g / 2½ oz
2 tbsp	Flour	2 tbsp
1⅓ cups	Milk	325 ml / 11 fl oz
	Grated nutmeg	
1 cup	Grated gruyère cheese	125 g / 4 oz
2 tbsp	Crème fraîche	2 tbsp

1. Remove the leaves and hairy choke from the artichokes. Peel the hearts with a knife, rubbing with lemon juice as you go along, so that they do not discolor. Cook the artichoke hearts in boiling salted water for 30-40 minutes or until the point of a sharp knife will go through them easily.
2. Meanwhile, chop the ham. Chop the mushrooms and moisten with a few drops of lemon juice to keep them white. Heat 2 tablespoons [25 g/1 oz] of the butter in a saucepan, add the mushrooms and cook until all the moisture has evaporated. Remove from the heat and mix the mushrooms with the chopped ham.
3. Preheat the oven to 400°F/200°C/Gas Mark 6.
4. Melt the remaining butter in another saucepan over a gentle heat and add the flour. Stir well, then gradually stir in the milk and a pinch of grated nutmeg. Season to taste with salt and pepper, and leave to simmer for 10 minutes over a low heat, stirring occasionally.
5. Add 4 tablespoons of the white sauce and about one-third of the gruyère cheese to the ham and mushroom mixture, and mix well. Fill the drained artichoke hearts with the mixture, and arrange in an ovenproof dish.
6. Add the crème fraîche and remaining cheese to the rest of the white sauce. Mix and pour over the artichoke hearts.
7. Place in the oven and bake for 15-20 minutes.

Endives au jambon

Endives [Chicory] with Ham

| | 00:10 | 01:10 | |

American	Ingredients	Metric/Imperial
12	Medium-sized heads of endive [chicory]	12
½ cup	Butter	125 g / 4 oz
2 tsp	Sugar	2 tsp
	Salt and pepper	
1 tbsp	Flour	2 tbsp
⅔ cup	Milk	150 ml / ¼ pint
1 cup	Crème fraîche	250 ml / 8 fl oz
½ cup	Grated gruyère cheese	50 g / 2 oz
	Grated nutmeg	
12	Thin slices of cooked ham	12
12	Thin slices of gruyère cheese	12

1. Remove the damaged leaves from the endives [chicory]. Using a pointed knife, remove the hard part from the base of the leaves by hollowing out the center. Wash and drain.

2. Melt 2 tablespoons [25 g / 1 oz] butter in a thick-bottomed saucepan. When it froths, add the endives, sugar and salt and pepper to taste. Leave to cook over a gentle heat for approximately 40 minutes. The endives are done when they are slightly browned and the point of a knife can pass through them easily.

3. Meanwhile, melt 1 tablespoon butter in another thick-bottomed saucepan. Add the flour and cook, stirring, for 1 minute. Remove the saucepan from the heat and gradually add the milk, continuing to stir. Return to the heat and cook, stirring, until thickened. Add the crème fraîche, half of the grated gruyère, a pinch of nutmeg, and salt and pepper to taste. Leave to cook for 5 minutes over a gentle heat, stirring continuously.

4. Preheat the oven to 425°F / 220°C / Gas Mark 7.

5. On each slice of ham, place a slice of gruyère and then a braised endive. Roll up the ham which should go right around the endive. Arrange the rolls in a buttered ovenproof dish. Cover them with the sauce and sprinkle with the remaining grated gruyère.

6. Bake for about 30 minutes. Serve in the cooking dish.

Endive (chicory)

Amuse-gueule saucisse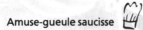

Sausage Cocktail Snacks

	00:20	00:10 to 00:15
	plus thawing or making pastry Makes 32	

American	Ingredients	Metric/Imperial
14 oz	Puff pastry	400 g / 14 oz
8	Cocktail sausages [chipolatas]	8
	Cayenne pepper	
1	Egg	1

1. Preheat the oven to 450°F / 230°C / Gas Mark 8.
2. Roll out the pastry ⅛ in / 3 mm thick, and cut out pieces which will *just* wrap around each sausage.
3. Lightly sprinkle the sausages with cayenne pepper and wrap each of them in a piece of pastry. Dampen the longest edge with water and press to seal. Coat the rolls with beaten egg. Cut each pastry-wrapped sausage into 4.
4. Arrange on a baking sheet and bake for 15 minutes. Pile them in a dish and pierce each of them with a toothpick. Serve hot.

Croûtes du skieur

Ham and Cheese Pudding

	01:00	00:15

American	Ingredients	Metric/Imperial
¼ cup	Butter	50 g / 2 oz
1 tbsp	Oil	1 tbsp
6	Slices of bread, ½ in / 1 cm thick	6
6 tbsp	Dry white wine	6 tbsp
6	Thin slices of cooked ham	6
1 tbsp	Vinegar	1 tbsp
7	Eggs	7
2 cups	Grated comté or similar cheese	250 g / 8 oz
2 tbsp	Crème fraîche	2 tbsp
	Grated nutmeg	
	Pepper	

1. Heat the butter with the oil in a frying pan. Add the bread slices and brown on both sides.
2. Place the bread in one layer in an ovenproof dish and moisten each with 1 tablespoon of the wine. Cover each with a slice of ham cut to the same size.
3. Heat 2 in/5 cm of water in a saucepan and add the vinegar. Break 6 of the eggs, one at a time, into a ladle and plunge the ladle into the boiling water. When all the eggs are in the water, remove from the heat, cover and leave to poach for 3 minutes. Remove eggs and place them in a bowl of warm water.
4. Preheat the broiler [grill] to high.
5. Remove the eggs and drain on a cloth. Cut off the excess white to give a regular shape. Place an egg on each slice of ham.
6. Mix together the cheese, remaining egg and crème fraîche. Add a pinch of nutmeg and pepper to taste. Pour this mixture over the eggs in the dish.
7. Place under the broiler and cook for 5 minutes.

Beignets de jambon cru

Ham Fritters

American	Ingredients	Metric/Imperial
	00:15	00:25
1 cup	Water	250 ml / 8 fl oz
6 tbsp	Butter	75 g / 3 oz
	Salt	
1 cup	Flour	125 g / 4 oz
4	Eggs	4
1 (5 oz)	Thick slice of smoked ham	1 (150 g / 5 oz)
2 tbsp	Blanched almonds	2 tbsp
	Oil for deep frying	

1. Bring the water to a boil in a saucepan together with the butter and a pinch of salt. Add the flour all at once. Mix vigorously with a wooden spoon until the dough comes away from the sides of the pan. Remove the pan from the heat. Add one egg and mix thoroughly, then add another egg and mix. Continue adding eggs, incorporating each thoroughly before adding the next.
2. Cut the ham into small cubes and mix into the choux pastry, together with the almonds.
3. Heat oil for deep frying to 345°F / 175°C.
4. Take a teaspoon of the pastry and drop into the oil, using another spoon to loosen the pastry ball. Continue adding balls of pastry to the oil, cooking about 10-12 at a time. Cook the fritters for 6 minutes or until they are well browned.
5. Drain the fritters on a plate lined with paper towels, and serve hot.

Rissoles

Savory Meat Turnovers

American	Ingredients	Metric/Imperial
	00:30 plus chilling Makes 12	00:30
½ cup + 2 tsp	Butter	125 g / 4 oz + 2 tsp
2 cups	Flour	250 g / 8 oz
1	Egg yolk	1
	Salt and pepper	
½ lb	Boneless veal shoulder	250 g / 8 oz
½ lb	Boneless pork shoulder	250 g / 8 oz
1	Shallot	1
1 tbsp	Chopped fresh parsley	1 tbsp
3 oz	Cooked ham	75 g / 3 oz
	Oil for deep frying	

1. Cut ½ cup [125 g / 4 oz] of the butter into small pieces and leave to soften at room temperature. Mix the flour with the egg yolk and a pinch of salt in a bowl. Add the pieces of butter, and mix rapidly to a dough. Roll the dough into a ball, and chill for about 1 hour.
2. Chop the veal and pork finely. Peel and chop the shallot. Melt the remaining butter in a frying pan and add the meat, shallot and parsley. Brown for about 15 minutes. Allow to cool. Dice the ham and stir into the meat mixture.

3. Heat the oil for deep frying to 345°F / 175°C.

4. Roll out the dough to a thickness of ⅛ in / 3 mm, and cut out 12 rounds with a diameter of 4 in / 10 cm.

5. Put 1 tablespoon of the meat filling on one side of each pastry round. Moisten the edges of the pastry, and fold it over into a turnover, pressing the edges to seal.

6. Put the rissoles into the hot oil and fry them for about 15 minutes or until golden, turning them over occasionally. Drain on paper towels. Serve hot, with tomato sauce.

Empanadas

Spicy Beef Turnovers

00:30
plus thawing or making pastry

00:15 to 00:18

American	Ingredients	Metric/Imperial
¾ lb	Puff pastry	350 g / 12 oz
2	Eggs	2
⅓ cup	Raisins	50 g / 2 oz
¼ lb	Lightly salted bacon	125 g / 4 oz
2	Onions	2
1	Green pepper	1
1 lb	Ground [minced] beef	500 g / 1 lb
1 tbsp	Tomato paste [purée]	1 tbsp
2 tbsp	Chopped green olives	2 tbsp
	Sugar	
1 tsp	Dried thyme	1 tsp
	Tabasco sauce	
	Salt and pepper	

1. If using frozen pastry, set it aside to thaw. Hard-cook one of the eggs for 10 minutes in boiling water. Drain, run under cold water and remove the shell. Chop the egg.

2. Put the raisins to soak in warm water.

3. Grind [mince] the bacon together with the peeled onions. Put this mixture into a saucepan over a moderate heat and cook, stirring frequently, until the onions are soft and transparent.

4. Core, seed and dice the green pepper. Add to the saucepan and cook until the pepper is softened.

5. Add the beef, turn up the heat and cook quickly until the meat is browned and crumbly. Pour off excess fat.

6. Remove from the heat and add the tomato paste, the drained raisins, chopped green olives, chopped egg, a pinch of sugar, the thyme and 10 drops of tabasco. Add salt and pepper to taste and blend thoroughly.

7. Return to a medium heat and leave to simmer for 10 minutes, stirring frequently. Leave to cool.

8. Preheat the oven to 425°F / 220°C / Gas Mark 7.

9. Roll out the pastry to a thickness of ¼ in / 5 mm. Cut out 6 rounds using a saucer and a small pointed knife, and roll them out into oval shapes.

10. Cover half of each oval with one-sixth of the cooled stuffing. Dampen the edges of the pastry with water, and fold the pastry over the filling to form a turnover. Press with a fork to stick the two edges together. Glaze the pastry with the remaining egg, beaten.

11. Bake for 15-18 minutes. Serve hot, warm or cold.

Grenouilles sautées

Sautéed Frogs' Legs

◁▭▭▷ 00:05
plus soaking

00:15 to 00:20

American	Ingredients	Metric/Imperial
24 - 36	Pairs of frogs' legs (according to size)	24 - 36
2 cups	Milk	500 ml / ¾ pint
	Salt and pepper	
6 tbsp	Flour	6 tbsp
¼ cup	Oil	4 tbsp
1 cup	Butter	250 g / 8 oz
1	Garlic clove	1
3 tbsp	Chopped fresh parsley	3 tbsp

1. Cut off the feet if necessary and place the frogs' legs in a mixing bowl. Pour over the cold milk, and add salt and pepper to taste. Soak for 30-45 minutes.

2. Drain the frogs' legs and coat them in the flour. Shake to remove excess flour.

3. Heat half the oil and 2 tablespoons [25 g / 1 oz] butter in a large frying pan. When it starts to smoke, put in about half of the frogs' legs – just enough to cover the bottom of the pan. They can be quite close together but not on top of each other. Cook until golden brown on both sides, turning carefully to keep them intact. Remove with a slotted spoon.

4. Add another 2 tablespoons [25 g / 1 oz] butter and the remaining oil to the pan. When hot, put in the remaining frogs' legs and brown as before. Drain.

5. Wipe out the frying pan. Melt the remaining butter in the pan over a low heat and add all the frogs' legs. Cook gently for 3-4 minutes.

6. Peel and finely chop the garlic. Sprinkle over the frogs' legs with the parsley and salt and pepper to taste. Toss briefly and serve hot.

Grenouilles à la provençale

Frogs' Legs Provençal

◁▭▭▷ 00:20

00:10

American	Ingredients	Metric/Imperial
24 - 36	Pairs of frogs' legs	24 - 36
	Salt and pepper	
6 tbsp	Flour	6 tbsp
6 tbsp	Oil	6 tbsp
5	Garlic cloves	5
1	Bunch of fresh parsley	1
2 cups	White bread crumbs	100 g / 4 oz
6 tbsp	Butter	75 g / 3 oz

1. Season the frogs' legs with salt and pepper. Roll them in flour and shake to remove the excess. Heat the oil in a large frying pan. Add the frogs' legs and cook on one side for about 5 minutes, then turn them and brown for a further 5 minutes on the other side.

2. Meanwhile, peel and chop the garlic. Wash and chop the

parsley. Mix the bread crumbs with the garlic and parsley.
3. Arrange the frogs' legs on a serving dish and keep hot.
4. Pour off the oil from the frying pan. Melt the butter in the pan and when it froths, add the bread crumb mixture. Stir for several seconds, then sprinkle over the frogs' legs. Serve very hot.

Escargots de Bourgogne

Snails with Garlic Butter

	01:00		00:30
	plus standing time		

American	Ingredients	Metric/Imperial
2 oz	Shallots	50 g / 2 oz
2	Garlic cloves	2
1 lb (2 cups)	Butter, at room temperature	500 g / 1 lb
2 tbsp	Chopped fresh parsley	2 tbsp
	Salt and pepper	
72	Canned snails with shells	72

1. Prepare the snail butter: peel and finely chop the shallots and garlic. Mix with the butter. Add the parsley and mash the mixture with a fork to blend thoroughly. Season to taste with salt and pepper.
2. Drain the snails. Drop them into a pan of simmering water and cook for 5 minutes. Drain, cool with cold water and drain again.
3. Put a pat of snail butter in each snail shell. Put the snails in the shells and fill with the rest of the snail butter.
4. Leave the snails in a cool place for 24 hours so that they absorb the flavor of the garlic butter.
5. Preheat the oven to 325°F / 160°C / Gas Mark 3.
6. Arrange the snails on snail dishes and put in the oven. Bake until the butter has melted and the snails are piping hot.

Escargots
du domaine d'Auriac

Fresh Snails Casseroled in Wine

	00:45 plus soaking	02:30 to 03:30	

American	Ingredients	Metric/Imperial
240	Small fresh grey snails	240
2½ cups	Vinegar	600 ml / 1 pint
2 cups	Sea salt	500 g / 1 lb
	Flour	
3	Onions	3
5	Cloves	5
1	Bottle of white wine	1
1 tsp	Juniper berries	1 tsp
1	Bouquet garni	1
1	Bunch of fresh parsley	1
2	Garlic cloves	2
¼ cup	Butter, at room temperature	50 g / 2 oz
¾ lb	Cooked ham	350 g / 12 oz
3 tbsp	Olive oil	3 tbsp
1 cup	Tomato paste [purée]	200 g / 7 oz
	Salt and pepper	

1. Let the snails fast for two weeks. Tip them into a bowl and sprinkle with the vinegar, sea salt and a handful of flour. Leave them to soak for 2 hours.

2. Wash the snails under cold running water, rubbing them with your hands.

3. Drop the snails into a large pan of boiling water and blanch for 2 minutes. Drain well.

4. Peel one onion, stud with the cloves and put in a cooking pot. Add the white wine, juniper berries and bouquet garni. Put the snails in the pot and add enough water to cover. Bring to a boil and simmer for 2-3 hours.

5. Chop the parsley. Peel and crush the garlic. Mix into the butter with a fork. Set aside.

6. When the snails are cooked, drain them, reserving the cooking liquid. Remove them from their shells and remove the intestine. Set them aside. Strain the cooking liquid.

7. Peel and chop the remaining onions. Chop the ham. Heat the olive oil in a flameproof casserole. Add the chopped onions, ham and tomato paste. Cook until the mixture is lightly browned, then stir in the snail cooking liquid.

8. Add the snails, parsley butter, and salt and pepper to taste. Simmer for a further 30 minutes. Serve hot.

Bouquet garni and juniper berries

SOUPS

SOUPS

Guidelines

Vegetable stocks and broths

Soak dried legumes and pulses in water for several hours, then put them in fresh cold water to cook. Lentils are an exception to this rule, since they are not normally soaked.

Thicken soup when necessary with a spoonful of instant mashed potato flakes.

Beef or poultry stocks and broths

Try to make your stock the day before it is needed so the fat will have time to rise to the surface and solidify. You will be able to remove it in this form easily by drawing a skimming ladle or spoon over the surface.

Bouillon or stock cubes are often very salt, so keep this in mind when you are seasoning your soup.

Puréed vegetable soups

Wash the vegetables carefully to remove any dirt, but do not leave them to soak or they will lose most of their vitamins and mineral salts.

Raw vegetables will cook more quickly if you first mince them in a food processor. Remember that the flavor of garlic, shallots, onions and leeks is intensified by mincing so reduce the proportion of these foods accordingly. Process the vegetables once again after they have been cooked.

Croûtons

For best results, use stale rather than fresh bread. Toast croûtons instead of frying them for a healthy result. If you must fry croûtons, use only a little butter or oil and brown them over a gentle heat.

Leftovers

Save vegetable peelings (making sure you have scrubbed the vegetables first) and the water in which they have been cooked to make an economical basis for soups.

Making a bouquet garni

Used to flavor soups and broths, a traditional bouquet garni consists of a fresh or dried bay leaf, several sprigs of fresh parsley or parsley stalks (with stems and roots) and a sprig of fresh or dried thyme, all tied together with kitchen thread. Try a selection of different herbs and flavorings for variety — tarragon, marjoram, basil, sage, fennel, oregano, rosemary or dried lemon and orange rind for example — or even a little celery or the green part of a leek.

Consommé

Consommé

This is a beef or chicken broth from which the impurities have been removed, thereby making it perfectly clear.

	00:10 plus cooling		01:40	

American	Ingredients	Metric/Imperial
2 quarts	Beef or chicken broth	2 l / 3½ pints
1	Carrot	1
1	Leek	1
1	Large celery stalk	1
2 - 3	Fresh chervil or parsley sprigs	2 - 3
1	Fresh tarragon sprig	1
4	Very ripe tomatoes	4
1 lb	Chopped meat	500 g / 1 lb
1	Egg white	1
	Pepper	

1. Cool the broth in the saucepan until the fat has set on the surface. Remove this fat using a skimming spoon.

2. Peel the carrot. Trim the leek and celery and slice them all finely. Chop the chervil, tarragon and tomatoes.

3. Mix together the vegetables, herbs, chopped meat and egg white. Add a little pepper and then a little water.

4. Pour the whole into the saucepan containing the broth and warm over a very gentle heat, scraping the bottom of the saucepan so that the egg white does not stick. Leave to cook gently for 1½ hours without stirring.

5. When the mixture froths and rises in the pan, skim off the fat and froth with a ladle, and leave to cook once again.

6. Strain the consommé through a fine sieve. All that now remains to be done is to season it in various ways.

Cook's tip: you can flavor your consommé by adding a liqueur glass of sherry when you are about to serve it.

Potage Saint-Germain

Cream of Split Pea Soup

🔪	00:10		01:15 🥘
American	**Ingredients**		**Metric/Imperial**
5	Leeks		5
1	Celery stalk		1
3	Onions		3
¼ cup	Butter		50 g / 2 oz
2 cups	Split green peas		500 g / 1 lb
2 quarts	Water		2 l / 3½ pints
1 cup	Crème fraîche		250 ml / 8 fl oz
	Salt and pepper		
	Croûtons for serving		

1. Trim the leeks and celery. Peel the onions. Chop all the vegetables roughly. Melt the butter in a large saucepan and add the leeks, onions and celery. Cook over a low heat until golden brown.
2. Add the split peas and water. Bring to a boil and leave to cook for 1 hour.
3. Purée the soup in a blender or food processor until smooth. Return to the saucepan.
4. Add the crème fraîche. Bring to a boil and simmer for 15 minutes. Add salt and pepper to taste. Serve hot, sprinkled with croûtons.

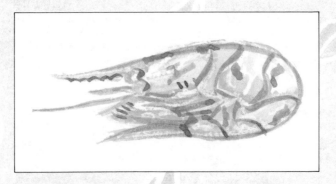

Potage aux tomates

Tomato Soup

🔪	00:10		00:45 🥘
American	**Ingredients**		**Metric/Imperial**
1 lb	Tomatoes		500 g / 1 lb
3	Potatoes		3
1½ quarts	Beef broth		1.5 l / 2½ pints
	Salt and pepper		
	Chopped fresh chervil or parsley		

1. Peel the tomatoes (first plunging them in boiling water for 10 seconds) and potatoes. Chop the tomatoes and potatoes.

2. Place the tomatoes, potatoes and broth in a large saucepan and bring to a boil. Add salt and pepper to taste. Simmer for 45 minutes.
3. Purée the soup in a blender or food processor until smooth. Reheat if necessary.
4. Serve hot, sprinkled with chervil.

Bisque de crevettes

Creamed Shrimp [Prawn] Soup

00:25   00:30

American	Ingredients	Metric/Imperial
2 lb	Large raw shrimp [prawns]	1 kg / 2 lb
1	Large onion	1
2	Medium-size carrots	2
2 tbsp	Oil	2 tbsp
6 tbsp	Butter	75 g / 3 oz
2 tbsp	Cognac	2 tbsp
1	Bay leaf	1
1	Fresh thyme sprig	1
1	Fresh parsley sprig	1
	Salt and pepper	
	Cayenne pepper	
2 cups	Dry white wine	450 ml ¾ pint
2 tbsp	Tomato paste [purée]	2 tbsp
1 quart	Fish stock	1 l / 1¾ pints
3	Egg yolks	3
1¼ cups	Crème fraîche	300 ml / ½ pint

1. Rinse the shrimp and drain. Peel the onion and carrots and chop finely.
2. Heat the oil and butter in a wide saucepan over a brisk heat. Add the shrimp. As soon as the shells become red, pour on the heated cognac and set it alight immediately. Add the onion, carrots, bay leaf, thyme and parsley. Add salt and pepper to taste and a touch of cayenne pepper. Leave to cook for 5 minutes, stirring frequently.
3. Remove the shrimp and set aside. Add the wine to the pan, cover and cook over a gentle heat for 15 minutes.
4. Add the tomato paste and stir well. Cook for a further 10 minutes over a gentle heat.
5. Remove the thyme, bay leaf and parsley and discard. Add the fish stock to the pan and bring to a boil. Simmer for 5 minutes.
6. Meanwhile, peel the shrimp.
7. Purée the soup and shrimp in a blender or food processor until smooth. Taste and adjust the seasoning.
8. Place the egg yolks in a soup tureen with the crème fraîche and mix thoroughly with a sauce whisk. Gradually whisk in the puréed soup.
9. Serve immediately.

Vichyssoise

Chilled Leek and Potato Soup

	00:30 plus chilling		00:30

American	Ingredients	Metric/Imperial
4	Leeks, white part only	4
4	Onions	4
3 tbsp	Butter	40 g / 1½ oz
5	Potatoes	5
1½ quarts	Chicken stock	1.5 l / 2½ pints
⅔ cup	Crème fraîche	150 ml / ¼ pint
	Salt and pepper	

1. Clean the leeks and chop finely. Peel the onions and cut into thin strips. Melt the butter in a saucepan, add the leeks and onions and cook for about 15 minutes over a gentle heat. Do not allow the vegetables to brown.
2. Peel and thinly slice the potatoes. Add to the pan and cook for 3-4 minutes, stirring continuously.
3. Bring the chicken stock to a boil. Add the vegetables and leave to cook for about 15 minutes or until the potatoes are tender.
4. Purée the soup in a blender or food processor until smooth, then strain through a fine sieve. Leave to cool.
5. Add the crème fraîche and whisk vigorously, then add salt and pepper to taste. Chill until ready to serve.

Soupe aux lentilles

Lentil Soup

	00:15 plus soaking		02:00

American	Ingredients	Metric/Imperial
1¼ lb (2½ cups)	Lentils	625 g / 1¼ lb
1½ lb	Smoked pork shoulder [collar bacon]	750 g / 1½ lb
2	Carrots	2
2	Leeks	2
1	Onion	1
2	Cloves	2
6 tbsp	Butter	75 g / 3 oz
2 quarts	Water	2 l / 3½ pints
1	Bouquet garni	1
	Pepper	
2½ cups	Milk	600 ml / 1 pint
6	Slices of french bread	6

1. Soak the lentils in water to cover for 4 hours. If necessary, soak the pork in water to cover to remove excess salt.
2. Peel the carrots. Trim the leeks. Dice the carrots and leeks. Peel the onion and stud with the cloves.
3. Heat half the butter in a saucepan. Add the carrots and leeks, cover and cook gently until softened. Add the water,

onion, bouquet garni, drained lentils and pork, and pepper to taste. Cook over a gentle heat, covered, for 1¾ hours.

4. Remove and discard the bouquet garni. Remove the shoulder of pork.

5. Purée the soup in a blender or food processor until smooth and pour back into the pan. Add the milk and heat, stirring. Taste and adjust the seasoning.

6. Toast the french bread slices. Put the remaining butter into a soup tureen, pour the soup on top and serve immediately, with the toasted bread.

Cook's tip: if you want to serve the pork with the soup, select a piece weighing at least 2¾ lb / 1.25 kg and extend the cooking time by 30 minutes.

Potage aux haricots blancs

White Bean Soup

	00:20	03:00
	plus cooling	

American	Ingredients	Metric/Imperial
1 cup	Dried navy [haricot] beans	250 g / 8 oz
1	Bouquet garni	1
1	Onion	1
1	Garlic clove	1
5	Celery stalks	5
2	Leeks, white part only	2
4	Large tomatoes	4
¼ cup	Butter	50 g / 2 oz
	Salt	
2	Egg yolks	2
	Garlic croûtons for serving	

1. Rinse the beans, place them in a large saucepan and cover with cold water. Cover the pan and bring very slowly to a boil (taking at least 45 minutes). Remove from the heat and allow to cool until lukewarm.

2. Drain the beans and put them back into the pan. Cover with plenty of fresh boiling water. Add the bouquet garni, peeled onion and peeled garlic clove. Return to a boil and leave to cook for about 1 hour or until the beans will crush easily.

3. Meanwhile, trim and chop the celery and leeks. Chop the tomatoes.

4. Melt half the butter in another saucepan. Add the leeks and celery and cook until softened. Stir in the tomatoes and leave to cook over a low heat for about 50 minutes.

5. When the beans are cooked, remove and discard the bouquet garni and onion. Purée the beans and liquid with the tomato mixture in a blender or food processor until smooth. Return to the saucepan.

6. Add salt to taste and bring to a boil, stirring well.

7. Mix the egg yolks with the remaining butter and 2 tablespoons of the soup. Add to the soup in the pan and heat through, stirring. Do not boil any further.

8. Serve with garlic croûtons.

Potage Crécy

Carrot Soup

American	Ingredients	Metric/Imperial
4	Carrots	4
4	Medium-size potatoes	4
3	Turnips	3
2 quarts	Cold water	2 l / 3½ pints
	Salt and pepper	
5	Shallots	5
⅔ cup	White wine	150 ml / ¼ pint
½ cup	Butter	125 g / 4 oz
	Croûtons for serving	

1. Peel the carrots, potatoes and turnips and cut into small pieces. Put into a saucepan and add the cold water, and salt and pepper to taste. Bring to a boil and simmer gently for 30 minutes.

2. Meanwhile, peel the shallots and chop finely. Pour the wine into a small frying pan and add the shallots. Bring to a boil and reduce to one-third over a moderate heat.

3. Cut the cold butter into pieces the size of a walnut. Add them all at once to the shallots, beating with a whisk. Cook, stirring, over gentle heat until the mixture is pale and thickened.

4. Purée the soup in a blender or food processor until smooth. Return to the saucepan.

5. Gradually stir in the shallot-butter mixture and leave to cook for a further 20 minutes over a gentle heat. Season to taste.

6. Serve in a soup tureen accompanied by croûtons.

Potage au cerfeuil

Chervil Soup

American	Ingredients	Metric/Imperial
2 lb	Potatoes	1 kg / 2 lb
2 cups	Cold water	500 ml / ¾ pint
	Salt and pepper	
1	Large bunch of fresh chervil	1
½ cup	Crème fraîche	125 ml / 4 fl oz
¼ cup	Butter	50 g / 2 oz

1. Peel the potatoes and quarter them. Place in a saucepan and cover with the cold water. Add salt to taste. Bring to a boil and leave to cook for 20 minutes.

2. Meanwhile, rinse the chervil and shake well to drain. Cut it very finely with a pair of scissors.

3. Purée the potatoes and liquid in a blender or food processor until smooth. Return to the pan. Add the chervil, and salt and pepper to taste. Cover and infuse for 2 minutes off the heat.

4. Add the crème fraîche and butter and heat through without boiling, stirring with a whisk. Serve immediately.

Soupe de poissons

Fish Soup

🔪 00:20		🍲 00:40

American	Ingredients	Metric/Imperial
1	Porgy or scup [sea bream]	1
3	Small ocean perch [gurnards]	3
2	Whiting	2
6	Small red snappers or mullet	6
3	Slices of eel	3
6	Small sea bass	6
1	Onion	1
1	Leek, white part only	1
5 tbsp	Olive oil	5 tbsp
6	Garlic cloves	6
1	Fresh fennel sprig	1
1	Fresh thyme sprig	1
	Pared rind of 1 orange	
	Salt and pepper	
2 quarts	Water	2 l / 3½ pints
½ tsp	Saffron powder	½ tsp
1	Sliced french loaf	1
1 cup	Grated gruyère cheese	125 g / 4 oz

1. Ask your fish merchant to clean and scale all the fish. Cut the porgy, perch and whiting into slices. Peel and thinly slice the onion. Trim and thinly slice the leek.

2. Heat the olive oil in a large saucepan. Add the onion, leek, heads and tails from the larger fish, 4 garlic cloves (unpeeled but crushed), fennel, thyme and orange rind. Add salt and pepper to taste. Cook for 3-4 minutes, then cover with the water. Bring to a boil and leave to cook for 20 minutes.

3. Preheat the oven to 350°F / 180°C / Gas Mark 4.

4. Strain the soup. Return the strained soup to the pan and add the saffron, eel, perch and porgy. Bring to a boil over a brisk heat, then simmer for 5 minutes. Add the rest of the fish and leave to simmer for a further 5 minutes.

5. Meanwhile, rub the bread slices with the remaining garlic, peeled and halved. Discard the garlic. Sprinkle the bread with the cheese and arrange the slices on a baking sheet. Bake for 3-4 minutes or until the cheese has melted.

6. Arrange the fish on a warmed serving dish. Serve the fish with the soup and slices of french bread.

Potage velouté au cresson

Cream of Watercress Soup

⌦ 00:10		00:30 ⌫
American	**Ingredients**	**Metric/Imperial**
1	Bunch of watercress	1
2 - 3	Potatoes	2 - 3
2 tbsp	Butter	25 g / 1 oz
2 quarts	Water	2 l / 3 ½ pints
	Salt	
½ cup	Crème fraîche	125 ml / 4 fl oz
2	Egg yolks	2
	Croûtons for serving	

1. Remove any damaged leaves from the watercress and rinse well, changing the water at least 3 times. Reserve a few nice leaves to decorate the soup. Drain the remaining cress in a salad basket.
2. Peel and slice the potatoes. Melt the butter in a large saucepan. Add the potatoes and cook for 5 minutes. Add the cress and cook until it is soft.
3. Cover with the water and add salt to taste. Bring to a boil and simmer for about 30 minutes.
4. Purée the soup in a blender or food processor until smooth. Return the soup to the saucepan and reheat.
5. Mix the crème fraîche with the egg yolks in a small bowl. Stir in some of the hot soup, then add this mixture to the remaining soup in the pan. Heat through, stirring, but do not boil.
6. Garnish with the reserved watercress leaves and serve the soup accompanied by croûtons.

Gratinée lyonnaise

Onion, Bread and Cheese Soup

⌦ 00:15		00:20 ⌫
American	**Ingredients**	**Metric/Imperial**
4	Large onions	4
¼ cup	Butter	50 g / 2 oz
⅔ cup	White wine	150 ml / ¼ pint
1 quart	Water	1 l / 1¾ pints
	Salt and pepper	
6	Slices of stale bread	6
2 cups	Grated gruyère cheese	250 g / 8 oz
1	Egg yolk	1
⅔ cup	Madeira wine	150 ml / ¼ pint

1. Peel and thinly slice the onions. Melt the butter in a saucepan. Add the onions and cook until light brown. Add the wine, then dilute gradually with the water. Add salt and pepper to taste and leave to simmer gently for 10-15 minutes.

2. Preheat the oven to 425°F / 220°C / Gas Mark 7.

3. Dice the bread. Half fill a deep round ovenproof dish with the diced bread and cover with a layer of grated cheese. Pour the onion soup over the bread. Scatter over the remainder of the cheese.

4. Place in the oven and bake for 15-20 minutes.

5. Beat the egg yolk and madeira together. Mix with a little of the soup and pour back into the remaining soup. Stir well and serve.

Consommé Belle-Hélène

Consommé with Eggs and Milk

	00:05	00:15

American	Ingredients	Metric/Imperial
3 cups	Cold broth	750 ml / 1 ¼ pints
1	Egg, separated	1
¼ cup	Ground rice	4 tbsp
3 cups	Milk	750 ml / 1 ¼ pints
1	Egg yolk	1
½ cup	Grated gruyère cheese	50 g / 2 oz

1. Remove the layer of fat from the broth using a skimming spoon. Heat the broth in a saucepan.

2. Beat the egg white in a bowl. Pour it in a trickle into the hot (but not boiling) broth. Stir gently until the egg white has solidified. Pour the whole through a strainer into a clean saucepan. You have now made what is referred to in culinary terms as a 'clarification.'

3. Return the consommé to the heat. Mix the ground rice with the cold milk, and when the consommé begins to boil, add the rice mixture, stirring thoroughly. When it boils for a second time, lower the heat and leave to simmer for 10 minutes.

4. Mix the egg yolks with 1 tablespoon cold milk in a soup tureen. Pour in the consommé, stirring continuously. Serve the consommé with the cheese.

Watercress (Cream of Watercress Soup)

INDEX